John Atwood

The Pilgrimage of a Pilgrim Eighty Years

John Atwood

The Pilgrimage of a Pilgrim Eighty Years

ISBN/EAN: 9783337293925

Printed in Europe, USA, Canada, Australia, Japan

Cover: Foto ©Lupo / pixelio.de

More available books at **www.hansebooks.com**

THE PILGRIMAGE

OF A

PILGRIM EIGHTY YEARS.

BY

JOHN ATWOOD,

Veteran Fisherman of Cape Cod,

Born in Provincetown, at 12.20 P. M., December 26, 1811.

BOSTON.
PUBLISHED BY THE AUTHOR.
1892.

Dedicated to

Young America.

THE AUTHOR'S PROSPECTUS.

This book contains a great variety of novel subjects not to be found in any other book now in print.

The author flatters himself that his path to wisdom has never before been trodden by any man of learning.

Hoping my friends and readers will find it smooth and level to the end,

I remain your humble servant,

JOHN ATWOOD.

ATWOOD ON THE UNDERSTANDING.

A CONUNDRUM, OR RIDDLE.

What five tribes or nations when named express the whole understanding of man?

Whoever solves this riddle first shall receive double the price of this book as a prize for his wit.

JOHN ATWOOD.

What the wise man, Zophar, said to Job:

Canst thou by searching find out God? Canst thou find out the Almighty unto perfection?—Chapter xi., verse 7.

It is as high as heaven; what canst thou do? deeper than hell; what canst thou know?—Verse 8.

The measure thereof is longer than the earth, and broader than the sea.—Verse 9.

Elihu's instructions to Job.—Chapter xxxv:

Look unto the heavens and see; and behold the clouds which are higher than thou.—Verse 5.

If thou sinnest what doest thou against him, or if thy transgressions be multiplied, what doest thou against him?—Verse 6.

If thou be righteous what givest thou him? or what receiveth he of thine hand?—Verse 7.

Thy wickedness may hurt a man as thou art; and thy righteousness may profit the son of man.—Verse 8.

Of God's great power in the leviathan, his answer to Job, chapter xli.:

Canst thou draw out the leviathan with an hook? or his tongue with a cord which thou lettest down?—Verse 1.

Canst thou put an hook into his nose? or bore his jaw through with a thorn.—Verse 2.

FREE DISCUSSION

Is like the air we breathe. If we have it not we die mentally.

> Let two wrestle together the question to solve,
> If it be heaven, earth or hell,
> Let them test it well.
> If it be God, devil or man,
> Let them do the best they can.
> Whether they be aged or in youth,
> Let nothing stop them but the final truth.

CONTENTS.

CHAPTER X.

9

PREFACE.

It will not be expected of me to write a book free from errors at my age of life, and without a common school education.

Therefore my readers will make due allowance for all errors which may be discovered.

My motto is "Truth," and therefore I shall hew to. the line, although the chips fly in my face.

But I will make an effort to lay before my readers some things which will be new to them.

If I succeed in presenting one idea or truth, in each subject which I purpose to treat, not heretofore known by some of my readers I shall thereby reach the standard at which I aim.

As the subjects upon which I purpose to write are various I hope to be able to furnish many facts never before seen in print.

Unknown facts ought to be very few and far between.

Of course such statements of fact as I shall lay before you, claiming that they were hitherto unknown, must be original (not before made public), whether they concern natural history, science, or theology.

I shall make only such statements as can be

10

demonstrated by my rule of the triangular square, where one positive will give two negatives, and the two negatives will prove the one positive.

This problem has never before been advanced.

It applies equally to the present, and to the future, and will prove all I claim for it.

It is an eye-opener.

You have to-day only two parts of the problem of the creation, and therefore your history of that event is not complete, but you are at sea adrift, as Paul was on his voyage to Rome.

I must apologize to my readers for imposing upon them the relation of a dream and vision in the first chapter, but I hope they will forgive me as it relates to the spiritual part of my life; and as spirituality in the early ages was the foundation of all religions, when young men dreamed dreams and old men saw visions.

Now the power of dreams has become wonderfully less. Realities have taken their place. Science, that brilliant star, has risen in the West, and become the Goddess of Liberty, the indicator of man's freedom, our star the first to dawn on our hemisphere.

Old stars are growing dim, and whereas all stars which have arisen in the East (the star of Bethlehem, of Egypt, and of Chaldea) have disappeared, our star hath grown to womanhood, and has put on the matrimonial robe and wedded the god of power, and obeyed the command of our creator to multiply and replenish the earth. ·

They have fulfilled their mission in part, as we see a goodly number of little stars, and the family is still increasing and shedding light over the whole world.

Our Venus, the goddess of liberty and beauty, is our star. We are the people, and our government is of the people, and for the people, and by the people.

Quite a large portion of the glorified earth is ours, with its sunshine and rain. We shall ever live and move and have our being.

We should be thankful for our good fortune. It is wonderful.

When I look back eighty years and reflect on what science and art have done I am astonished. But I am not looking backwards for information, as the ministers do. It is for reflection.

I look ahead and see the boy Young America grown to manhood, and strong and healthy. May his strength and shadow never be less.

"Eternal Boyhood" should be the motto of nations. Ours has come to stay, while others have passed away.

Selfishness and sin have put out the eyes of progression. Man has looked away up beyond the clouds for information and guidance (but he didn't get it), and then sung "All things are vain here below." Is this the doctrine to teach Young America? (Not a bit of it.)

I am sorry for our preachers, for many of them are good men and may be mistaken in their calling, having been taught from their infancy the old doctrine of Egypt, which has been remodelled from that language, now lost and dead. It was the "Eternal Boyhood of Individual Men," which proves itself false now.

Daily reflections like the following selections from Pythagoras are worth more than gold :
What have I learned, where have I been?
From all I have heard, from all I have seen,
What know I more that's worth the knowing?
What have I done that's worth the doing?
What have I done that I should have shunned?
What duty have I left undone,
Or into what new follies run?
These self inquiries are the road
That leads to virtue and to good.

Whether one knows much or little, it is of the greatest importance to know what one knows and why he knows it.

The principal knowledge which one should possess is to be cognizant of the fact that all power outside of the physical organism is derived from the non-equilibrium of the sun's heat and light by friction and the polar forces, which are dark and cold, which contracts; whereas the heat of the sun, that subtle manager of electricity, expands, which fills a vacuum on the earth, which is the cause of the movement of the air to restore an equilibrium.

This omnipresent good is all the life there is outside of organism; yea, with its dear sun, it evolves all organisms.

This process requires no intelligence, but is self-existing and eternal.

Individual organism and development constitute the secondary life, with power to move and transmit its like and control the elements in part.

Man being the microcosm or omniscient power will

continue to discover new wonders, and pass on, leaving millions of other wonders unexplored.

So there will always be something new to be learned by mankind. Happy thought.

In reference to the first creation of our earth I wish to say to my readers that the first chapter of Genesis contains an account of the whole formation of the earth and all things thereon, as I have described in this book.

The Bible account varies just a little from the original, just enough to suit the wants of the age when it was copied. I will give you the variation :

In the beginning the gods formed the earth (that is, the air and the sun), whose genial warmth spread over the face of that mighty deep and expanded that liquid of life. So vapor arose and formed into clouds, and swept over the dry land, to water the earth and produce vegetation. (This we find to be true, even know.)

As the sun warmed the ocean and the wind gave it motion, which is active life, the fish were formed by the evolution of inert matter as stagnated water. And the birds of the air were formed in a similar manner.

As you know, insects are evolved from pure water, which has become stagnated, and launched forth into the air with their wings spread.

I have taken pure water just descended from the clouds, and by the aid of the sun and wind have formed mosquitoes. There had not been a single parent mosquito within one hundred miles for six months.

My readers must know that all life and motion are derived from the non-equilibrium of the sun and the polar forces.

They also know that heat expands and cold contracts, a fact which causes a vacuum on the surface, the sun being the positive center of heat to expand above 32 degrees, and the two poles the negative below.

This proves my theory, as there cannot be a center without two opposites; neither can there be two opposites without a center.

The sun and air are the cause of all animal and vegetable organization and life; yet they both at times destroy life.

But no candid person will say that they do it with malice aforethought, or that they have intelligence.

I have endeavored in this work to separate truth from falsehood. Therefore I have found two distinct creations, thoroughly antagonistic. The first is founded on facts. The second is founded on dreams.

The first book of the creation is the first book of Genesis, with slight variations.

The second book is called the book of Job, and placed next to the book of Genesis in the first Bible's chronology. Thirty-nine chapters, with a little variation or addition, comprise the book.

The first two and last chapters are not a part of the original book, or dialogue, that shows what relationship man is to God.

On those two books I rest my case as regards the creation and ownership of this earth.

My opponents can have all the other books of the

15

Bible, with Josephus and all the alterations that have been made in it, which are many. And they prove themselves all alterations in the books, and to have been designed by some person.

I want my readers to carefully go through the book of Job for themselves. It belongs to the first creation. It has five known characters and one supernumerary God, but no devil in it. Man was all it needed.

But Job did not write the book, neither he, nor his friends, nor his enemies. It was written by other men.

In the twenty-third verse of the nineteeeth chapter Job is represented as saying:

"O that my words were now written! O that they were printed in a book!"

And the thirty-fifth verse of the thirty-first chapter:

"Oh . . . . that mine adversary had written a book."

Very few of the books which comprise the Bible were written by the persons whose names are given as the authors.

So it will be very important for you to know whose essay you are reading; where, when, and by whom and for what purpose it was written, and whether it has been garbled to suit the capricious whims of some person or persons.

A very respectful friend to Truth and Humanity.

JOHN ATWOOD.

INTRODUCTION.

I COMMENCED without a school education. I have arranged the following subjects to the best of my ability, but you will find it all there, and fully setting forth my theory, although somewhat jumbled together.

This book gives a life-search of the author, with hundreds of references of ancient and middle ages and modern times (including many Bible citations) extending down to the present day, and from the sublime to the ridiculous; giving the theory of the creation as set forth in the Bible, by Hugh Miller, Charles Darwin, and by John Atwood.

I have found the missing link in the chain of creation, and shackled on the anchor of Truth and Hope.

The problem is solved and the triangle is completed. All right.

By the rule of trigonometry, simple and compound, I am able to finish the creation up to the present period of time by three problems, Evolution, Revolution, and Dissolution.

The two positives will give the negative that has

been made known and fully demonstrated by mathematics and the four rules of navigation.

But how to find the two negative parts have never been made known.

This I shall do.

And that will prove what Copernicus said when he was about to die: "The world still moves." He was a wise man, and recanted and saved his life, or the good·men would have killed him, as they did Bruno.

Do the wise men of to-day think they know all there is to be known?

Men will come after us and call us fools, and will not miss the mark when compared with themselves.

I shall prove what the first death is, and tell who has had his part in the first resurrection; and what the second death is, and demonstrate it; and also what the past was, what the present is, and what the future will be.

Don't marvel, dear reader. I shall give you a poem from a play that was presented in Athens five hundred years before the Christian era. Also, a letter written by Theophilus to the Blessed Virgin Mary, and her answer.

I shall refer to some very curious fish stories that came within my experience, and will vouch for their truthfulness; and shall also explain how it is they discount the fish stories of old.

Truth is stranger than fiction.

I presume many of my readers are not aware that there is a species of fish which nurses its young from a bottle.

There is no animal below the human child that is made to draw its milk from a bottle except a fish.

I shall give the name and classify the kind of fish, and explain how it is done—a wonder of creation.

I shall give you some selections from the sayings of wise and good men, and some from other men, and you shall have the privilege of culling as you think proper.

Go not in the way of bad men.

Any man who teaches a theory that he cannot demonstrate and prove true to simple men and women is a knave, or bad man.

If his silly-billy stuff injures any person, he ought to be punished.

Let it be distinctly understood that the Bible has affixed to it two distinct creations.

And whereas the Christian world has jumbled them together and made hodge-podge of the whole book, I shall separate them and give the proof as it has never before been given to man.

A glance at the past is sufficient.

Now look ahead for happiness to come—not backwards; for I shall prove that all who have lived cannot live again with the same identity they once had.

You are living now, so you need not fear the second death.

One world at a time is sufficient.

One life is all that belongs to you or me.

Arm yourself and proceed.

Dispute every word if you are able to bring the proof.

The ownership of this earth is the question at issue.

Resolved, That man is the first and rightful owner of this planet, according to the account of the first creation as given in the first chapter of Genesis.

I take the affirmative undeniably, and just creation where man has dominion and ownership of all below him.

My opponent, Rabbi Helctiah, picks up a new creation in the second chapter, by a new creator, whom he styles "Lord God," who makes man, the first of all created beings, full grown, and purely immaculate, and calls his name Adam.

I consider him the biggest still-born child ever imposed on mankind.

My opponent declares that the earth is the Lord's and the fulness thereof, but he shows no title.

I dispute the premises.

I declare that men while they are on this earth own it, occupy it, and have dominion over it, as God promised they should.

Possession is nine points of law.

My opponent, that arch-priest, will tell you that your soul is not your own. He will seem to bring proof from his record by quoting such passages as, " Ye are not your own, but bought with a price."

You must infer that his Lord is in the slave trade, buying up souls.

But in perusing this work you will not believe what I say, but watch your colleague and question him concerning his own sayings. You will need no evidence of mine to convince you of facts unless you have wholly embraced idolatry.

The fool hath said: " There is no God," but that is not true.

The God I introduce I shall prove to you.

The air is the only Omnipresent Invisible.

The sun is the Omnipotent visible God.

The father and son of immortal matter, self-existant, co-equal, co-eval, and co-eternal—the same yesterday and forever—our creator and sustainer.

Man is the third person in the trinity, making the only omniscient God, and these three are one God.

Man is the microcosm or personification of the true God.

And here and now I shall prove what God is by known rules of logic, for what he is makes him a God.

And that none know there is any God unless he knows what God is, for what he is makes him a God.

I shall have no need to prove to my readers that the air is the only thing that can be everywhere, and form a new body there. And as it is with forms so it must be with identities; they come like the seasons, have their day and pass on, that other seasons may come.

So with man's identity.

Reader, man as matter is immortal, but men as individuals, like you and me, come from dead, inert matter, by the power of God.

It is impossible that identities which have had a beginning can be eternal or immortal. There can be but one eternal God, and that is matter without personal form and void of intelligence.

So no act of cruelty can be charged to God by ignorant men.

I shall also prove to my readers what the first death is, and what the first resurrection from the dead is, and who they are that have their part in the first resurrection, on whom the second death can have no power.

I shall prove to you that there is but one individual life, and that their are two deaths.

By the square of reason.

Nowhere else nor by any other person is this so fully set forth and truly demonstrated.

I will show you a mystery, or a truth.

We do not live when identity of form and will power are dead.

In our sleep every night it is by our God of imagination being in tune for life, but where has the will power of man gone? Into nonentity for the time being; where the woodbine twineth.

I shall refer you to your own Bible creation for evidence in addition to the scientific and demonstrable philosophy, which is all-sufficient to convince any man who has no creed to hamper him.

In succeeding chapters I shall endeavor to show my readers what God is in order that they may not have to round out seventy years as I did before they find out the true God.

If you endeavor to find the true God by inquiring of theologians, I can recommend you to thirty-two different ones who represent every point of the compass. They will tell you that their course is right, and that all others are wrong.

The first will say: "Here! Here! Pay your fare, and I will ticket you through and check your baggage."

The second will say: "The gospel is free. Our Christ is the only redeemer."

The third will tell you that none will be saved unless they believe in his Jesus.

The fourth will tell you that all will be saved whether you believe or not; that Christ bought you with His blood.

This gives the best assurance of any of the 146 different religious denominations or sects in the United States, says the Philadelphia Record.

All of them have a different method of reaching heaven.

What nonsense it is to have so many ways when there cannot be but one straight road to that place.

My way is different from them all, and I don't ask you to believe, but read on and dispute every point I make.

You have no need to dispute any of the thirty-two that are steering by one compass,—which is the same Bible,—because they dispute each other; so that settles the question.

None of them can be right. it must seem.

. Is it possible those men are sane, or can there be so many different gods.

Unless men made them so, we conclude that man made the gods, all but the one true God, and He don't write on paper, nor instruct men to do so.

That is a voluntary power with men, and they have abused it.

CHAPTER I.

I ENTERED my career in this life as a fisher boy at the age of eight years. At nine years I was cook of schooner Seaflower. At the age of ten years I was cook of schooner Porpoise.

I had early Christian instruction, such as it was. My father and mother were pious, or they thought they were, and I thought so too, of course.

I received no school education, living at a distance from town. My father taught me that to know God, and to know Him aright, was life eternal.

I thought that was worth looking for. I commenced my search for God. It was up hill and down vale the first twenty years. I thought I was wicked, although I never did anything that was bad.

At the age of fifteen I dreamed that I died and went up to heaven. The door was opened, and I saw many that I had been acquainted with, and some of them I knew had not been very good while they were on the earth. But my sentence was: "Depart, ye cursed, into everlasting punishment; I know you not." I demurred, and claimed that there were some there not so good as I was; but I was hurled towards that unmentionable place, which so frightened me that I awoke and rejoiced that it was only a dream.

25

I shall never forget those horrible twenty years I lived without hope and without God in the world.

But at the age of twenty I found there was a universal God and a heaven, and a Saviour, who had died to save all mankind, and that He would do it.

" Ye are not your own, but you were bought with a price," were His words, so I was told.

Of course he would protect His property. Then I was Happy with a capital H. So I went on my way rejoicing.

My father said he was just as sure there was a hell as that there was a heaven, but I did not think so then. I am satisfied he was right in regard to a local heaven and a local hell; but enough of this foolish doctrine. I pass it by, and let it go.

And I go on my way rejoicing. I was happy, and continued so until I was seventy years old. But I was not quite satisfied that I knew God aright, because to know God aright was to know what God was. To know there was a God He must be made manifest to my senses.

Behold, I had a vision, and I heard a voice. I listened and heard these words: " O ignorant man, that thou art, thou hast been looking for me these sixty years. O foolish man, if I must reveal myself to thee, I am the air you breathe; I am always with you; I am in you, and you in me. Thou canst have no other omnipresent God but me. I watch over you in your sleep. I go out with you and come in with you. Let not vain babblers deceive you. I will explain myself to you.

" Shall mortal man be more just than God? They

come and go like the seasons, the trees, and the stars. They are made of that same immortal matter; but the stars of today are not the stars that always were, although of the same immortal matter, but will pass away as nebulous matter, and form new stars in the universe. So there is always an infinite number of stars to man, but not the same; nor are the men who live now the same men who lived before, but they are of the same immortal matter. So you see that I, your God, am without form and invisible, but I and my sun that you see are the creator of all forms.

"Be still, and know that we are gods.

"Visible and invisible, immortal matter, always the same, yesterday and today, the same immortal matter, without beginning or ending. Time with us is ever one eternal Now.

"But I manifest myself in man's flesh, with an organized brain, that men may know what God is."

God's almighty power shows what He is. He can pass unobserved, or he can manifest his power. Our God and His Christ are without malice aforethought, but the creator and mover of all worlds and beings.

Here I desire to offer a short prayer to our God that he will assist me and enable me to finish this great work of revealing Him to men, in as few words as it can be done, for we are not commended for much speaking or reviling.

The truth is simple, and will prevail in the twentieth century.

"O Thou whom no eye can see, nor mind comprehend; thou immutable, omnipresent essence of life, the creator and mover of all worlds and beings, we adore, bless and thank thee for the gift of thy dear sun, our saviour, the Logos of to-day, in whose light and warmth we ever live and move and have our being. Thou art the same yesterday, to-day, and forever, our God and His Christ. Amen."

I am no sectarian. I make no war on any sect or creed. I respect all men if they are good. I have friends in most all of the prevailing denominations, and they all look alike to me. They are men and brothers, and they treat me as such. I accord to every man the right to his own belief if he is honest in it.

My friends are good men and true, and I wish them a long and happy life, and there I leave them with their God.

Whatever they have sown they shall reap. I have lived a long and useful life, and never have injured any one intentionally who did not deserve it badly, and but very few at that, only to punish them for their bad deeds to me.

And now all of my enemies are dead. I don't know that I have one enemy in the world. If there be one it is because he is not willing for me to enjoy my own opinion and state what I honestly believe or know, the same as he claims for himself. Be merciful to man and render to others the same as you would wish them to render to you.

I have no enmity toward any man. I only make war with principles that I consider wrong and injurious to the human family, and give in return what I consider to be true and beneficial. In life such has been my experience. In life I have no axe to grind, nor any one to fear in this life; and all I have to say to my readers in this chapter is to be good, and learn for yourselves, as I have done.

My name is recorded in the Lamb's Book of Life by the recording angel as one who loves his fellow-man; and the rewarding angel has placed it with the blessed as one who has had and is having his part in the first resurrection. It is happiness to me to know that it will be rest and peace with me when I go. I bid you all good-by, as I shall probably soon leave you. Farewell, dear friends.

CHAPTER II.

PSYCHOLOGY is the science that teaches wisdom. It never drives a person insane, and he that possesses it will never die a fool.

He may die a knave if he makes a wrong use of it, as some do.

It is the hidden mystery. But few know it. I have been asked many times to teach it, and offered money double the amount I paid. But I did not consider that the people were ready for it. It has too much power to be put into the hands of many, even now. St. Paul, you know, after he was educated was not considered worthy to receive that mystery which was handed down through the Leviticus priesthood. None were permitted to receive it except they were of the Tribe of Levi, and had studied for the ministry.

In receiving it I pledged my most sacred honor as a man that I would not teach it for a less sum than I paid for it. And I pledged to myself that I would not teach it for money.

You will bear in mind that this art, which comes by the laying on of hands, came from Egypt, and we have two branches of it that have been handed down to the present period a secret.

Let it be distinctly and always borne in mind that every iota of the Christian religion is of Egyptian origin. Peter, the foundation of the Catholic church, was an Egyptian Jew by the name of Simon the son of Simon, a magician, at Alexandria. Simon was a fisherman on the river Niger, as I have stated in another chapter.

Jesus was educated at Alexandria, and at that great school received the secret that gave him such great power.

Josephus called him the Egyptian false prophet who came to Capernaum and collected some thousands of fishermen, mariners and common laborers. He claimed He had superhuman power, and led His army up on the Mount of Olives to be instructed of God, the same as Moses claimed.

Then he attacked the Romans, was defeated, and fled.

He taught all His disciples, but some of them were not worthy.

Take your Bible and study Peter's character.

The wise Catholic priests have forbidden the common class to use the art, but you occasionally read of their practicing it.

Paul calls it the Holy Ghost by the laying on of hands. He received it through the Peter clan. He was so highly educated and had such confidence in his abilities that he entered into an argument on the merits of this matter with Peter, who was comparatively uncultured.

But with all of Paul's great learning Peter was more than his equal in the debate which ensued.

They were hale fellows well met as far as character and natural abilities were concerned.

Read your Bible as a man ought to read it, and see if I have not given Paul his true character. In another chapter I have given only a few of his evil deeds.

The Jewish rabbis have this secret, but they are superstitious, although they are progressing, which is more than I can say of our religion. It does not admit of any progression by man, and the greatest wonder is that man is as good as he is, after being taught that false Pagan or Indian doctrine of a Great Spirit in the form of a man that fills the whole earth and is a person, but is not man.

Such has caused man to transmit to his offspring for thousands of years that falsehood. We know that like begets like, and that children resemble their parents very much. And how can it be otherwise?

I here give you a demonstration of facts by the science that I call Psychometry, science of mind; Biology, the means whereby the unknown Psychology is found.

This is my definition of the words.

Man is a microcosm, representing all things below him, with a double brain, where the seat of life is located. The cerebellum, or back brain, is the seat of life; and the cerebrum, or the front brain, is the generator of all thought. The knowledge, the identity of man is of but short duration, and as Paul refers to it after the manner of men when he says "I die daily," I suppose he called the whole twenty-four hours a day; and he went to sleep every day and forgot himself, and was dead as far as the senses were concerned, and if he had not awakened he would have been eternally dead.

This faculty was given us to instruct us in our life that there would be an eternal sleep, at last when the cerebellum, or back brain, ceases to act in our sleep, or unconscious state. You know that the cerebrum is controlled as regards life wholly by the cerebellum, or back brain, which runs the machine entirely when we are unconscious; but when it is worn out or ceases to act we don't have to die—we are already dead.

It is a mistake to think that we were born to die— we were born to live. That is the object of life. Don't forget it.

CHAPTER III

I NOW desire to make a note by way of explanation regarding the two characters I met in my pilgrimage.

The first was a very good and wise god, who made everything in a scientific and systematic manner.

He was the god of the Chaldeans.

The history of the creation was given some thousand years before the Israelites' Lord God commenced the creation, beginning with the second chapter of Genesis and ending with the third chapter.

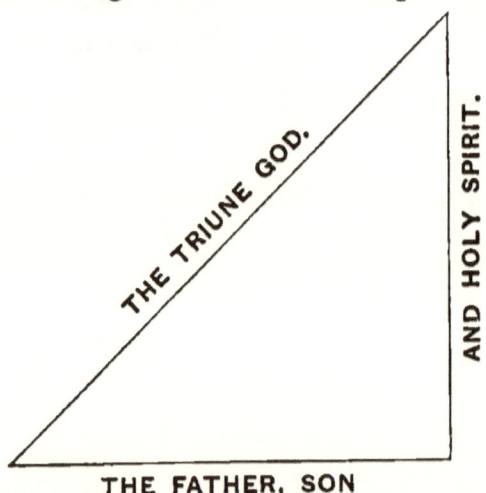

THE FATHER, SON

In getting wisdom get understanding, for without this you are as sounding brass or as tinkling cymbal.

But my readers are supposed to be wise men, and do not need all this caution.

As this book is to be dedicated to wise men, I want you to start fair and run fair. I recommend you to read the first two chapters in your Bible so that you will be prepared to understand the mysteries that I shall point out to you verbatim, with a single reference to Job and the writer of the said book, which was written long before Israelite Adam was made of dust.

All that was original of the dialogue, or psalm, written in the book of Job was taken from the Chaldean account by Hellekap, the learned Jewish rabbi, during the seventy years' captivity of the Jews in Babylon, and committed to memory by that designing priest.

After the exit from Babylon he wrote the book called Job, and that dialogue, prefixing two chapters and adding one chapter to make it Israelitish and foolish.

My object is to teach my pupils something that they can't forget, whether it is foolish or otherwise. My experience has been long in reading the written Bible, as well as the old open book of Reason, the bible of God.

Every man who has extracted a new truth, or brought to light an old truth, and has demonstrated it to mankind, has written a sentence with the finger of the mind in that book. But there are plenty of blank leaves which cannot be wholly written over while man inhabits this planet. He is ever learning, and never able to come fully into the knowledge of the full truth.

In the first creation we have not a very extensive chart of that great province of Chaldea. We can give you the number of its cities and towns, which was ten, with the largest city that the world ever knew, that great and mighty city, Babylon, the largest city and comprised of the most refined people in the world; the others being city of Uz, city of Buz, city or town of Shu, of Naam, of Tem and Nod, Tema, Sheba, and Ophir.

These are the names of all the cities and towns given in the Bible. Daniel in his dreams wanders too much to be reliable.

The book of Job belongs to the people of the first creation. There are five characters as men and one supernumerary called god. It is a dialogue or parable, similar to that of the rich man and Lazarus, recorded in the New Testament, only that Job was the rich man and the devil smote him with sores; and Lazarus was the poor man, and God smote him with sores because he disobeyed the laws of his nature. But when he died God sent his angels and they took him and put him in Abraham's bosom, while the rich man went tumbling down to hell.

So it is not a man's good moral character that carries him to heaven, as Dives was better than Abraham and Lazarus according to Bible doctrine.

Let it be distinctly forever and eternally borne in mind that the world and all things in it were as recorded and completed in the first chapter of Genesis, and that the earth and everything thereon was given to man; not only once stated, but repeated and clinched.

Therefore the ownership of the earth is man's, which was given to him by the creator. I consider it an offence against God to contend that God owns all the earth when He has freely given us all things, and commanded His first people to write it down in a book, and here I give it to you.

I don't want to say what I think of those Jews who so falsified the words of the gods who formed the heavens, the earth and all the things thereon, and has so declared it by his presence.

Read the chapter. Don't be afraid to understand it. It will not hurt you to know the truth, though you may think it will.

I shall give you in another chapter some statements made by Daniel. In his dreamy state he is visionary. He speaks of the Kings of Babylon, of beasts, of rams' horns, great horns and little horns. But Daniel belonged to the second creation.

Read the first chapter of Genesis. That is my good God, every time, and the only true and living God there is to-day. He is your God, also.

So don't cry, as did Mary Magdalene at the sepulchre, "They have taken away my Lord, and I know not where they have laid Him."

Be patient. The true God is here, and He is ever mindful of your needs. This God gives you breath, while your machine is in order to receive it. And His son gives you light, warmth and life. Without that blessed life-giving and life-sustaining influence we could not live. It is our Father and His son who give us individual life.

Read the first chapter of Genesis, which follows, carefully, and you will find that the world and all created beings were made and pronounced good. And why should there be another creation necessary? I want you to read the second and third chapters, and note the contradictions of the account of the first creation, and you will notice that there were two persons created man—male and female. This God, or these gods, could not be an individual and be in everything and be somehere else at the same time. This is self-evident.

There is one point gained.

The sun is the centre force from which all light, heat, and living and moving power comes. This is self-evident.

This is another point gained.

That this God and his Christ are self-existent and eternal matter, no one can successfully deny. Should any one object I shall meet him with demonstrative philosophy.

That the combined matter of our earth consists of solids and liquids from which man was formed no sane man will attempt to deny. This matter is immortal and indestructible from which forms are made —man, the image and form of God, and the handiwork of the only God, personified and made manifest in the flesh through the two positives—by Evolution of inherent force in matter the form comes and is a person; by Revolution it moves and has an individual being, and is a part of the great God. And as it had a beginning so it must have an ending, therefore by Dissolution it passes away in gases to some secluded spot in the universe.

Now follows the first chapter of Genesis:

1 In the beginning God created the heaven and the earth.

2 And the earth was without form, and void; and darkness was upon the face of the deep. And the Spirit of God moved upon the face of the waters.

3 And God said, Let there be light: and there was light.

4 And God saw the light, that it was good: and God divided the light from the darkness.

5 And God called the light Day, and the darkness he called Night. And the evening and the morning were the first day.

6 And God said, Let there be a firmament in the midst of the waters, and let it divide the waters from the waters.

7 And God made the firmament, and divided the waters which were under the firmament from the waters which were above the firmament: and it was so.

8 And God called the firmament Heaven. And the evening and the morning were the second day.

9 And God said, Let the waters under the heaven be gathered together unto one place, and let the dry land appear: and it was so.

10 And God called the dry land Earth; and the gathering together of the waters called he Seas: And God saw that it was good.

11 And God said, Let the earth bring forth grass, the herb yielding seed, and the fruit-tree yielding fruit after his kind, whose seed is in itself, upon the earth: and it was so.

12 And the earth brought forth grass, and herb yielding seed after his kind, and the tree yielding fruit, whose seed was in itself, after his kind: and God saw that it was good.

13 And the evening and the morning were the third day.

14 And God said, Let there be lights in the firmament of the heaven, to divide the day from the night; and let them be for signs, and for seasons, and for days, and years:

15 And let them be for lights in the firmament of the heaven, to give light upon the earth: and it was so.

16 And God made two great lights; the greater light to rule the day, and the lesser light to rule the night: he made the stars also.

17 And God set them in the firmament of the heaven, to give light upon the earth,

18 And to rule over the day and over the night and to divide the light from the darkness: and God saw that it was good.

19 And the evening and the morning were the fourth day.

20 And God said, Let the waters bring forth abundantly the moving creature that hath life, and fowl that may fly above the earth in the open firmament of heaven.

21 And God created great whales, and every living

creature that moveth, which the waters brought forth abundantly after their kind, and every winged fowl after his kind: and God saw that it was good.

22 And God blessed them, saying, Be friutful, and multiply, and fill the waters in the seas; and let fowl multiply in the earth.

23 And the evening and the morning were the fifth day.

24 And God said, Let the earth bring forth the living creature after his kind, cattle, and creeping thing, and beast of the earth after his kind: and it was so.

25 And God made the beast of the earth after his kind, and cattle after their kind, and everything that creepeth upon the earth after his kind: and God saw that it was good.

26 And God said, Let us make man in our image, after our likeness; and let them have dominion over the fish of the sea, and over the fowl of the air, and over the cattle, and over all the earth, and over every creeping thing that creepeth upon the earth.

27 So God created man in his own image, in the image of God created he him; male and female created he them.

28 And God blessed them, and God said unto them, Be fruitful, and multiply, and replenish' the earth, and subdue it; and have dominion over the fish of the sea, and over the fowl of the air, and over every living thing that moveth upon the earth.

29 And God said, Behold I have given you every herb bearing seed, which is upon the face of all the earth, and every tree, in the which is the fruit of a

tree yielding seed; to you it shall be for meat.

30 And to every beast of the earth, and to every fowl of the air, and to everything that creepeth upon the earth, wherein there is life, I have given every green herb for meat: and it was so.

31 And God saw every thing that was made, and, behold, it was very good. And the evening and the morning were the sixth day.

CHAPTER IV.

THE whole truth of Evolution, Revolution and Dissolution at one grasp and deposited in a nutshell.

First, matter is immortal in whatever form it may be.

The sun is the cause of all life or motion, and is the living proof of visible matter without knowledge in itself.

The air is the invisible omnipresent matter without intelligence.

Those two forces by the power of Evolution are forming and moving all worlds and beings.

Reader, since your Bible was written it has been discovered that our earth is a true child and revolves around its mother—the center sun. This parent has a watchful care over her offspring, our earth, by the aid of our Father, who walks our earth without being seen by us; but in Him we live and move and have our being, and without His aid in providing for our wants our mother could not support her children and keep them alive.

Those I have named are our great-great-grand-parents.

I state to you in this chapter facts that are self-evident. Therefore they need no demonstrative evidence of mine to prove them.

You must be aware that our earth has a vacuum on its surface which is the cause of all motion.

As the burning sun strikes on our meridian and causes a powerful non-equilibrium between its heat .and the cold forces of the poles, so the wind rushes as though it had a mind to freeze all the water to the Gulf stream, that is, in the winter, when our mother is not so near us.

But it becomes spent and then its death is potent.

And then the south wind springs up, with warm rain, and rushes north, with seeming determination to melt all the ice clear to the north pole, but it becomes equalized before it gets there.

All these wonderful performances are certainly going on without any individual mind to conduct them.

I have fully proved in other chapters that there cannot be a personal omnipresent God outside of man,—and that man male and female—was evolved from inert matter, so far as intelligence and dead organism are concerned.

Our first parent was not made of the masculine gender alone, out of dust, without moisture, and full grown, according to Hugh Miller's theory, as I have said in other parts of this book.

Nor was he made from a monkey, whether full grown or otherwise, as Darwin has asserted.

But it was just as easy for the creative power called God or gods to create man in his ignorant and

44

barbaric state as it was to create the monkey, baboon, or any other animal.

The objection that I have to the Hugh Miller theory is that God, or Lord God, could not make man out of dust without liquid, and that it was square-handed to make a full-grown fool without having him grow up like all other animals.

The only objection to the Darwinian theory is that God, or gods, could not make men from monkeys and have the monkeys left as monkeys. It must destroy the monkeys as a race to make them into men. Then there could be no monkeys.

It was just as easy for the gods to make men after there own or a better image as it was to make them after the image of any other animal.

When our mother Earth was of proper age she produced man—male and female—and left off bearing, and delegated the right of production to her children, and they have carried on that work from generation to generation, even until now.

I ask the learned theologian who pretends to know all about God why He left off the creation when He had made the monkey, or when he had made Adam, full grown, and forbid him to know anything.

My friends, any of them who are ministers, can answer with safety, for they cannot answer more foolishly than thousands of others have done.

Why should God stop creating man—male and female—in their infancy, as other animals are and were created and commanded them to multiply and replenish the earth, and pronounce everything He had made good; and He created no Satan in his first creation.

And the gods created man in there own image, that is in the best image of all the animals which had been made—as it is set forth in the first chapter of Genesis, which gives the history of the whole creation of everything, and which was pronounced good.

Now put your thinkers at work and don't be befooled by me or any other person, for all the writing about God and the gods has been done by man, for God or the gods never wrote a word on paper since the formation of our earth.

It is wonderfully strange that men will be led away by designing priests, whose only aim is to keep people in ignorance of nature and nature's laws, when it is so plain that the universe is governed by law.

But as man is so selfish, and because he has been taught to believe what is erroneous, and so much money has been spent on him to fit him to be able to deceive the unlearned, and by so doing he is enabled to control the minds of many and make them believe that he has been inspired by an invisible God to write that imaginary God's will in the face of nature's unchangeable laws.

The fact is that the theologian has been deceived and has paid his money for it, and he means to get it back and a good living besides by dealing damnation around the land on those he deems his God's foes.

All doctrines are proved to be wrong by their contradictions of each other—all taken from one book and claimed by them all to be the word of God.

How any sane man in this age of intelligence can for one moment believe that any one of the many doctrines is right is a wonder to me.

And I find but few men within the age of reason, who are between 21 and 70 years of age, who really believe in experimental religion.

The time or period is fast approaching when men will be honest with themselves and come out of this visionary lethargy, so contradictory to all real truth.

This is rather hard for me to write because I have some friends who are ministers, and very excellent men they are as men. I am very sorry for them, as their trade compels them to say and do what they would not otherwise do; but it is all in the trade.

There are many truthful lawyers and honorable men outside of their profession, but duty demands of them that they make a strong effort to prove the criminal innocent, when they know he is guilty in their own minds. Some lawyers will not take the defence in a criminal case. (They have a conscience.)

My trade by which I got a living was a very deceptive one. I was a fisherman, and all fish are taken by deception or force, or by both combined. I could do it with a good will, and was called an expert at it.

But I never became a fisher of men, and never used my skill that way. I never wanted to catch men with guile as some other fishermen have done, although I had received and paid for my tuition of that monster art of deception called Electro-Psychology.

It is the two-edged sword of knowledge; it enables one to do good or bad, as his organization inclines him to do.

I am glad that I was born right, and do not need

47

to be born again ; and never expect to be, as one life is sufficient for one person, and as I do not agree with Hugh Miller or Darwin, and as they do not agree with each other, you will readily see that one of them must be wrong.

Well, they are both negative to me. I am the positive, and declare that they have not finished their work. So it is understood Charles Darwin did well as far as he went, but he left one link of the chain out, and that is the most important one, and is larger than any other. It is the shackle that connects the chain to the Anchor of Hope and Truth.

When he had finished all the links I do not see why he did not make the connecting shackle, instead of leaving that for me to do.

Well, I can do it.

Charles Darwin finished his chain when his God had made the monkey, gorilla, ourang outang, and baboon. There he was stuck.

I pick up his chain. It was well made thus far, but it has no shackle. It is just as easy for my God to make the shackle as it was to make the chain, if he took a little more stock, and of that he had plenty.

Reader, you have no right to say that God could not make man when He said or they said He did ; and we see him around as large as life, and plenty of little fellows who will grow into men.

Now the chain is complete, and I have shackled it to the Anchor of Life and Immortality.

The chain is strong, the anchor is sure and steadfast within the vale of our God's heritage, and we have become the omniscient God personified.

We know that matter is immortal, and all forms come and go, for it is impossible to be otherwise.

As I often say to my readers, there are three things to be considered, and I work by the rule of three, direct and compound, when the problem requires it.

The simple mathematical rule of the two positives of the square gives the negative every time, and in the compound rules of navigation the course and distance run give the latitude and longitude.

This was discovered long ago.

The trigonometry taught in your colleges has never gone beyond that; but I am going to show you and demonstrate what never before has been given to man to know,—or man has never declared it to my knowledge, viz., that by one positive of the square the two negatives are known. I shall give it in a subsequent chapter.

I hope my friends, the learned theologians, will not throw down this book with contempt because it was written by an ignorant fisherman who cannot spell correctly, nor write grammatically.

I want to remind them here again that the foundation of their religion—of which they boast so much—was promulgated by the ignorant fishermen of Galilee, who could not write at all, and that others wrote their stories as they were related to them.

Peter, James and John were the leaders of your gospel and the founders of your religion.

Matthew was a tide waiter and collected taxes from the fishermen, and might have written his book, as he had a little learning; but the three fishermen told their stories and other men wrote them.

John made his mark (X), and one book was called Mark.

Peter told his story, and alluded to Jesus; and they called the book Luke.

Theophilus wrote the gospel according to his idea of John, and called it the Gospel according to St. John. That surely means that John did not write it.

It was written by some other person long after John the fisherman was dead.

This John who could not write.

Your book says that Peter and John were ignorant men.

But he was the beloved disciple, and Jesus could trust him. He would not be as liable to violate the law as the others would. So he put his mother in his charge, and he was to be her son in his stead, and she to be his mother; and he told him that he should tarry on the earth till he came.

So says your book. I leave you to settle that part of the question, as I am dealing with your witnesses without cross-examination.

I asked a minister once at a Sunday school who wrote St. John's gospel when the question or lesson embraced the authenticity of the four gospels. I told him that it could not be John the Baptist, although he figured largely in the first four chapters, always as the second or third person; and it was not John the Revelator, the fisherman, son of Zebedee and Salome, of Capernaum. He agreed with me.

Then I asked him what John it was. As I was in search of knowledge I would be pleased to have him inform me, not knowing that there were any other Johns mentioned in the New Testament. He said he would tell me, but he has never done so.

About two years afterward I wrote to him asking if he would redeem the promise he made me in the Sunday school at Provincetown.

He did not answer for the best of reasons, viz., he could not.

I am certain he received my letter, as he resided in the same city (Malden), and was the Universalist preacher there at the time. Since then he has slid back to the first John's gospel, Baptism. This is going backwards, as well as looking backwards.

I suppose you have read Bellamy's book, "Looking Backward," for it is fair to suppose that everybody has read it, as fiction and dreams have reigned triumphant since the days of John the Baptist even until now. The gentleman's name is Babbitt, with the prefix "Rev."

I hope my sticking him on the Johns was not the cause of his backward movement, for surely I meant no harm in giving the true author of the book ascribed to John, nor in asking him what John it was. I listened to him several times. He was a very powerful speaker, with a tremendous voice.

But he run "shold," as we fishermen would say.

As I have mentioned Jesus and John the Baptist, I will present two letters written by your friends, long ago, and it is asserted that they are genuine, written by the persons whose signatures are attached to them. Of course, dear reader, your friends could not lie.

I have copies of the letters, said to be true by millions of learned men. I give you test copies of the originals. I find the first dated Paris, A. D. 1495, written by your gospel vendors, and of couse it must be true to all who believe in Hugh Miller's "Footprints of the Creator." The letters bear witness of being written in true ancient style, and are as here presented, written in the first century:

"The Epistle of the Blessed Ignatius to the Holy Virgin Mary, mother of our Lord Jesus Christ.

"To the Christ bearing Maria, her own Ignatius sendeth his compliments.

"You ought to comfort and console me who am a new convert and a disciple of your friend John, for I have learned things wonderful to be told concerning your Jesus, and am astonished at the healing; but I desire from my very soul to be certified immediately by yourself, who was always familiar and conjoined with him and privy to his secrets, considering the things I have heard.

"I have written to you other epistles also, and have asked concerning the same things.

"Farewell, and let the new converts who are with me be comforted by thee, and from thee, and in thee.

"AMEN."

The Blessed Virgin's answer:

"To Ignatius, the beloved fellow-disciple, the humble handmaid of Christ Jesus sendeth her compliments.

"The things which you have heard and learned from John concerning Jesus are true. Believe them; cleave to them; hold fast the vow you have made to

52

Christianity which you have embraced, and conform your life and manners to that vow; and I and John will come together and visit you.

"Stand firm in the faith; act manfully; nor let the sharp severity of persecution move you; but may your soul fare well and rejoice in God, your Saviour.

"AMAN."

CHAPTER V.

THIS chapter will treat of the immortality of the soul triumphant, or the difference between the immortal and mortal defined.

The immortal is without beginning of days or the ending of years.

The immortal God is all-powerful and ever present, self-existent and eternal, the same yesterday, to-day and forever, without variableness, or the shadow of malice or anger.

But the mortal god, man, is full of malice and anger. At times he is capable of doing good or bad, in accordance with his organization and subsequent development.

It has been and is now taught that there is only one God, consisting of three parts, a triune god—omnipotent, omnipresent, and omniscient. This is the Christian's God.

And now I shall endeavor to define the parts that go to make up the great God, our creator.

And I will say to my friends and readers that whatever their religious views may be as regards the future, it is all right with them so long as they do unto others what they would that others should do unto them when in like circumstances.

The more exalted views you have of your God and his heaven of rest or praise the more pleasant your dreams will be and the greater your happiness in this life in anticipation of another. You will never be disappointed.

All who believe in an angry God and think they are wicked and deserve to be burned in that visionary lake of fire and brimstone will receive their reward in bad dreams, and be like the troubled sea, continually casting up mud and mire in their minds.

I will make a few quotations from the Bible of sayings alleged to have been made by the wisest and best writers of that book—not that it is necessary, but it may better satisfy some of my readers who think all knowledge must come from (my theory is self-evident) the Bible.

Solomon says the righteous and the wicked are alike in death.

The king and the beggar lie down together.

There is no device in the grave.

Man dieth and goeth to his long home (that is, from whence he came).

The mourners go about the streets.

When dead men go about the streets and the mourners stay at home, then the order of nature will be changed.

Again, who knoweth that the spirit of man goeth upward and the spirit of the beast goeth downwards?

I could give hundreds of similar quotations, but it is not necessary.

Men know more to-day than Solomon did.

If they do not, then in what have they progressed?

We once existed and were without individual form, and devoid of intelligence, but a part of the immortal God.

We now exist in an organized form, with an intelligent brain, and become the omniscient God, or microcosm, and are still a part of the great whole.

Pope, in his "Essay on Man," says "all are but parts of one stupendous whole, whose body nature is, and God the soul" (that is the whole subject).

As I have described the immortal soul as eternally existing there must be an opposite soul that does not exist always, and that is mortal, and came into being with an organized form and a brain possessing a mind, or it could not have been known that anything ever existed. That mortal soul came from that unorganized matter which we call death.

Hence it arose from the dead, as we term death, and that must be the first resurrection, and we have the first individual life that preceded the second death. If there had not been an organized body possessing life there could not have been any second death. That is certain.

So there can be but one intelligent life for each individual, as everything that has a beginning must have an end, as I have before stated.

Our organization had a beginning; so it cannot be immortal. It is the matter that is immortal and ever changing from one thing to another, but yet the same immortal matter.

Every sane man must know that as the identity of himself came to him not long ago, so it must end in time, as it is impossible that there should be an increase in anything without a corresponding decrease to balance it; and if an intelligent spirit occupies any space then space would have been filled before our day, and we should have been blocked out.

As we are here, and living monuments from the first death, we are also sure that we shall pass into the second death, which can have no power to hurt or mar our feelings.

It is the struggle for life that causes pain, not death; that is the release from all pain.

We were not ushered into this world to die, as is often said. We were born to live, the machinery being in order, and to live as long as we can; and when we cannot live any longer we are already dead and at rest.

Eternal rest; blessed thought.

I consider life worth the living. This life of mine has been a great blessing to me, and not once have I regretted it.

It has been a happy life to me in my waking moments, and in my sleep, that temporary death, I have obtained that necessary rest that my identity required to keep it in repose for more useful work. It is the fittest that survives, all accidents excepted.

We are therefore assured that when this lifehood ends we shall all go to make up that lifehood of God, of immortal matter, where there is no pain (which for the want of knowledge we now call death).

CHAPTER VI.

TIME is only one eternal now. By this problem I demonstrate what never has before been made known, viz., that one known positive fact will give two negatives in the rule of trigonometry.

Now is positive time.

Past is negative—not in existence.

It also proves that there is a future that is a negative now, but will have an existence when it arrives and becomes a period of time.

All things come, and go; so with periods. They last while they exist, and no longer.

These things are facts, for I deal in facts only.

This problem applies to man's form as well as to other things.

It also applies to his identity as well. Every individual identity had a beginning, and will have an ending, all priestly doctrines or religion to the contrary notwithstanding, for what had a beginning must of necessity have an ending. I desire to impress this on your minds.

Our knowledge of ourselves is not immortal, but had a slow beginning in development a few years ago, and it will have an end in death when this machine is worn out. There our individual knowledge ends.

Matter is immortal.

Matter is eternal.

Matter is, was, and always will be the same.

Time and matter are eternal.

Matter is the god that always was and always will be; the same, to-day, yesterday, and forever.

It is impossible that there could have been a beginning without an end.

There cannot be an egress without there having been an ingress. Think of that.

All the priests, with their gods and devils, cannot make it otherwise.

Let any of the theologians prove there is a personal god outside of man who is omnipresent and it would take no prophet to foretell out fate.

A personal god who fills all space would not admit of another person. So the believers in a personal god are dumbfounded.

It is in perfect harmony with all nature that God is personified in man; that he is a microcosm, or representative God in man.

This earth is governed by law inherent in matter. I repeat this saying.

All bibles and ancient priests who lived and wrote books when men did not know that the earth was round, but thought it was flat, like a pancake, and wrote that the sun got up in the morning and laid down at night—such men who advocate this Bible theory, like Hugh Miller, are of no consequence to-day.

The problem of life and death is solved.

There is one personal life for every individual who has an identity, and no more.

Every person now living proves his existence. That is positive, and that proves that he arose from the dead, which to him now is negative; and as we shall die and pass into dead matter, from which we came, that proves the second negative, which occupies a position opposite to our present life.

So here and now I give the triune fact of Death, Life, and Death. There are two deaths; the first was inert matter whice sprung into our life, and was the first resurrection from the dead.

And there is the second death to be, which can have no power on our present life.

The said death is negative now, and is proven by the one single positive, Life.

Let the forty-five million of sectarians, or their representatives at Washington, prove one point of this triangle false, or even all of the one hundred and forty-five different sects do it, if they are able. Let them bring evidences that stand on their feet, and I will knock them asunder.

Truth is powerful, and it will prevail.

The fishermen of Galilee put out the eyes of wise theologians eighteen hundred years ago, and a fisherman of Cape Cod can do it now.

They tell you in the Bible that Jesus said that as Moses lifted up the serpent in the wilderness so shall the Son of Man be lifted up. (That is a fact.)

But how did Moses lift up the brazen serpent?

Now this is all the knowledge you have concerning it.

I know how he did it, but I shall not give it away here, but if any one wants to know, let him come to me and I will show him how it was done. So be it; so be it.

There were some miracles said to be performed by those fishermen apostles, but they were not miracles.

The principal apostles were fishermen. They told fish stories that probably were true. Peter, the chief, caught a fish with coined money in its mouth.

I don't dispute that. I have caught hundreds of fish with coined silver money in their mouths, both Spanish and American coin.

Peter caught only one; but then Peter's experience in the fishing business was small compared with what I have had during seventy years of my life.

He did not live half so long, and part of that time he was fishing for men.

The preachers professing to advocate the doctrine taught by Peter are better clad and wear shoes, whereas Peter went barefooted. They know more in one direction than he did, and less in another. He could not convince some of the people then without showing his Satanic art, as Moses had done before him.

But the apostolic doctrine now in vogue proves in one point to be true.

When Jesus was asked by His followers how men should know His true followers in after times, He replied:

" You will not believe me without I show you a miracle.

"But they will be strong-minded men. They can

61

take up serpents; they can drink the deadly poison, and do all the works that I do; yea, and more, they do it."

Because those who do do what Jesus did make their followers believe all the stories told of Him in the Bible, without any miracle, or even without any proof, except that magnetic or psychological power that the fishermen of Galilee possessed, by which bad men can do much evil to others, even to the taking of life, as has been done, which I have referred to in other parts of this work.

Good men can do wonders by the same art, as I have done, many times in a manner that astonished me.

I learned this art from a very highly educated teacher of the gospel of Jesus, before whom no preacher in this country could stand in argument. That was fifty years ago. I paid for my information, and it was worth all I gave for it, and a hundred times more, in my business, which required great skill in finding things that had been lost, which I did every time without employing a detective.

I was my own detective, my own lawyer, my own preacher, by the aid of this science, which is wonderful.

I have been requested to teach it, and have been offered very much more than I paid, but I refused to teach it for the reason that I did not think the people had arrived at the standard of morality and goodness which was necessary to make them worthy to receive it. This I have mentioned before.

I shall have occasion to refer to Saul and show you what effect it had on him.

As you know, he was taught in all the learning of the Jews at the feet of Gamaliel, a Jewish priest of great education. But when he was of age to receive the certificate given to the priests by Aaron, the Levite (Paul was also a Levite) he was thought to be too unstable and wicked to be entrusted with that sacred secret.

So he was given a license to go and persecuteth Christians, even unto death, and he did it with malice and anger, which was his nature. He killed James, the Just, son of Alpheus and the other Mary. James was called the Lord's brother, after the flesh. This wicked deed was done at Jerusalem.

I shall have occasion to refer to him after he was converted, as he was of great learning, and King Agrippa said unto him, "Paul, thou art beside thyself; much learning hath made thee mad."

Paul was Paul after all, and I shall refer to him as uttering the truth that exactly agrees with my theory of the resurrection, and swearing to it as truth, as no other man who is alleged to have written a portion of the Bible has done.

I receive the truth wherever I can find it, and as many of my readers put great confidence in Paul and his teachings I may score a point in exactly agreeing with him on the resurrection from the dead, although I might differ from him on other points. If a teacher teaches truth I receive it, although it might be Satan, the wisest and greatest teacher recorded in your Bible.

For it says that God delivered two of His children over to Satan that he might teach them not to blaspheme. This speaks well for his moral character and great learning, with liberty to teach. So be it, so be it. They were Philetas and Hymenæus.

I would say to my readers that the way to get knowledge is to hear the argument of your opponent.

I feel thankful that Adam ate the forbiddn fruit that enabled him to know good from evil, and transmitted that great blessing to us. I thank heaven for this boon, that preachers generally term the original sin. And some of them (very respectable and learned men) have declared that hell is paved with infants' skulls on account of this original sin.

Verily I must say that all who believe in such a personal God are insane on that point to a greater or less degree. If there be such a God I would say to him: "Drive me out of Eden when you please, but first let me partake of the fruit of the knowledge of good and evil. I want to be wise. I will risk the salvation or damnation it brings."

But listening to such preaching, which has but one side, is of but little value to the hearer. It is like the politician who reads his one-sided paper which spouts out its lies, all of which he sucks down as the truth. And of him who only goes to hear his own side expounded, what can he know that's worth the knowing, whether he be Republican, or Democrat, or Prohibitionist? He might as well be nothing.

This foolish and selfish habit that men have got into of hearing only one side of any question and then deciding in favor of it because they want it so, without any evidence being introduced by the other side, is like a certain Dutchman I once heard of who, when a lawyer had made his plea for the defence, said: " He is innocent, certain." But when the prosecuting lawyer was heard then he said; "He is guilty, sure."

I am indebted to my opponents for most all that I know, for I was born a "·nothing," and taught in the " know but little doctrine " for many years. But I thank the stars of glory which taught that one star differed from another star in light or glory, but that it took all the stars of heaven to complete the galaxy.

And so of men, with their multiplicity of thoughts. And are they not all entitled to a hearing? Hear them all, and embrace only that which is good. Try every man by his own standard.

If there is any man who has a theory of a god or gods that I have not heard or read of, I should like to hear or read it, if it is worth the hearing, or has any vim to it, whether it be Christian, Jewish, Mahometan, or Pagan, or any of those numerous sects, the most of which have passed away, with their gods and images, which will eventually be the fate of all personal gods. Those gods have fled, but man is here.

CHAPTER VII.

HERE are the first eight verses of the thirteenth chapter of Revelations, which will furnish food for thought to thinkers:

And I stood upon the sand of the sea, and saw a beast rise up out of the sea, having seven heads and ten horns, and upon his horns ten crowns, and upon heads the name of blasphemy.

And the beast which I saw was like unto a leopard, and his feet were as the feet of a bear, and his mouth of a lion: and the dragon gave him his power, and his seat, and great authority.

· And I saw one of his heads as it were wounded to death; and his deadly wound was healed: and all the worlk wondered after the beast.

And they worshipped the dragon which gave power unto the beast: and they worshipped the beast, saying, Who is like unto the beast? who is able to make war with him?

And there was given unto him a mouth speaking great things and blasphemies; and power was given unto him to continue forty and two months.

And he opened his mouth in blasphemy against

God, to blaspheme his name, and his tabernacle, and them that dwell in heaven.

And it was given unto him to make war with the saints, and to overcome them: and power was given him over all kindreds, and tongues, and nations.

And all that dwell upon the earth shall worship him, whose names are not written in the book of life of the Lamb slain from the foundation of the world.

John's predictions have not been fulfilled, and I thsnk they never will be, as there are so many who who are not travelling that road now.

The following article is from the "Open Court," and will be found to contain some interesting statements:

"The statistics of religion and theology, of late more accurately collected and recorded than ever before, give small encouragement to those who claim prosperity and predominance for the system founded on recognition of Jesus as the Christ.

"Of the 1,200,000,000 of the world's population, 390,000,000 are nominally Christian. Less than one-third of them, perhaps 110,000,000, are Protestants, and these Protestants declare the Christianity of the others to be seriously defective, both in regard to faith and practice. The Protestants in the United States number 30,000,000, but of these only 9,000,000 are church members or communicants, that is, Christian in the meaning assumed to be the correct one by the clergy and the churches. But since these 9,000,-000 of actual Christians are divided among forty-five sects, which seem to insist more on their distinctive and divisive peculiarities than either on the beliefs which they hold in common, or the purpose they pursue in common, they surely cannot have the efficiency of an army under a single leader. Their character as churches militant is shown rather by their contests with each other than by united warfare against the vice and ignorance everywhere around them. Holding very diverse and often opposite opinions, they all refer to the Bible as their rule, and as the only and sufficient rule of life and duty. And yet this assumed allegiance to the Bible, far from tending to unite the five varieties of Presbyterians, eight of Baptists and twelve of Methodists, actually helps to keep them separated. Investigation and criticism, though opposed by a majority of the clergy, are constantly tending towards still further division. Thus, contact with American ideas has caused division even among Roman Catholics; and the Episcopal church, ranked as one among the forty-five above mentioned, has its practical division into high, broad, low and reformed.

"Critical investigation, as I have said, is now pursued in all civilized countries more persistently than ever. Nevertheless, so far has clerical teaching effected a popular distrust of reason in reference to religion that an immense majority of the church membership in this country still hold firmly to beliefs which research, scientific and literary, has thoroughly disproved; such, for instance, as the unitary character and divine inspiration of the Old and New Testaments.

"If the foundation fails, what will become of the edifice? If the corner-stone crumbles, what will avail the claim that the building was founded on a rock?"

When I take a mental view of the past and behold man in his infancy, more helpless and ignorant than the brute creation, then I wonder and ask why did not God create man independent of all other beings, and I hear a low voice saying: "I did, but foolish man has made it otherwise. If they had followed my injunctions it would have been well; but my servant, Job, made a fool of himself, and went crazy, and brought evil on himself by disobeying my commands, and violating the law of his being, and brought on boils, as did Lazarus," spoken of in the parable of Dives and Lazarus.

Then I wondered again, and asked myself with all sincerity: "Does man really bring those diseases on himself, or does God send them on him to punish him, as many people contend?" He says he does not.

Then I marvelled, and put those two wonders of mine together as perpendicular and base as positives. Then I look. Then I figure, and then I find that those two wonders are equal to one hundred per cent. each, brought to feet is one hundred feet.

Now I have mastered the mystery. Here is the problem.

The two creations are supposed to equal 142 per cent., of which 42 per cent. take the first creation, and 100 per cent. take the second creation.

This applies to man, woman and child.

The above problem is figured by the rule of three, minus the fractions, either vulgar or decimal.

But when we take men within the age of reason, from 21 to 70 years, we find a large percentage embracing the true revelation, giving man's destiny.

I will give their percentage by the same rule.

In all Christian nations there is 59 per cent. of the said men who believe in the first resurrection, which is scientific and demonstrative, and has no Satan.

But there is but 41 per cent. of those who come within the said age, from 21 to 70, who believe in the second creation of devils and hell.

I care not what men say about it. Figures and problems don't lie. I am wandering about nature and God now, and as I wrote the wind came in squalls and the leaves blew around the house like so many sparrows. Then I stopped writing. I wondered that my opponent said that not a sparrow falleth to the ground without his father's notice.

Well, can't I help him out on this? Yes, I have, it is true. But it is my god, not his, and there is not a leaf that flies in the air, without head or wings, without my Father's notice.

Then he says it is written in his Bible that the Lord God of Israel told his children as warriors to go out and fight their enemies and there should not a hair fall from their heads. Well, then I wondered. Then I figured. I made a low estimate of the number of hairs that had fallen from my head and they amounted to 1,168,000, and I have plenty of hair left. I am not at all bald.

Then I concluded that this army of men were all bald. What other conclusion could I come to? My opponent is a truthful man, and I respect him very much. He declares that that was the word of his God.

That good prophet, Elijah, was baldheaded. So be it.

Then my friendly opponent says his father feeds the young ravens when they cry. There, don't say any more.

I have always considered ravens, crows, and English sparrows a pest instead of a benefit. And now, my friends, if your father feeds the young ravens and feeds the old hen hawks with chickens I must think you are a great deal better than your father.

Well, I believe in progression, and I know that you would sooner kill a hawk if it was stealing your chickens then you would feed it. Marvelous!

One more example. Among the ministers are many of my good friends, and very excellent men they are, too. I will quote from their great and wise preacher, who was King over Israel in Jerusalem.

What does he preach? He says that the great God who formed all things both the fool and the transgressor.

He also says the righteous live long on the earth, and that the wicked shall not live out half of their days. (Who will live out the other half?)

He says that the good man showeth favor and lendeth. He will guide his affairs with discretion. Surely he will not be moved forever. He shall be in everlasting remembrance. His heart is fixed trusting in the Lord.

Let us contrast your wisest and best preacher of the second creation with my most foolish and worst preacher of the first creation, Job.

71

Solomon was a wise man, with all his faults; and Job was a foolish and crazy man with all his riches.

Those wise and good men, his friends Eliphaz the Temanite, Bildad the Shuhite, Zophar the Naamathite, who were all very excellent men, were so closely copied by Solomon that it made him appear to be more than head and shoulders the superior of the great minds of his times. .

But I must tell you about Job, your patient man. Read his history. I call him the most impatient man who ever lived.

Read what he says in the twelfth chapter of the book which bears his name, wherein he censures the pretensions of his friends to superior knowledge. He says: "No doubt but ye are the people, and wisdom shall die with you."

I know that the wicked flourish like a green bay tree, and that the righteous man is cut off in his righteousness. These things are but illustrations of his power; but the thunderings of his voice who can understand?

Now God answereth Job through the mouth of Elihu, one of the four friends of Job, with this question: "Canst thou draw out the leviathian with a hook, or his tongue with a cord, which thou lettest down? Canst thou put a hook into his nose, or bore his jaw through with a thorn?"

You will remember that Elihu was a Buzite, and he buzzed Job out of his foolish nonsense.

Now you will understand that the book of Job was a Chaldean dialogue, with five characters, and one supernumerary called God.

But the whole book is a fiction. It was taken by the Jewish rabbi Helekiah from Babylon, when that people were dismissed from that great city because the inhabitants had no use for them on account of their worthlessness. They had so befuddled Job that they were glad to be relieved of their presence. Thereafter they were allowed to have home rule by spells, but lost it for good eighteen hundred years ago the second and last chapters not in the original.

A people so foolish as to harbor a God who will not let them defend themselves one-seventh of the time cannot be a nation long.

Poor Ireland is in the same boat.

CHAPTER VIII.

OUR visible father the Sun, our mother the Moon, and their children the Stars, are a happy family in the heavens. There is no imagination about this. They rule the day and night, and are not ashamed of their actions. They mete out that which is good generally to their children here below who are individually of but short duration—not long-lived like the children above, but have their day and time, and are gone.

The following is from the pen of Mr. W. Perkins of Kansas City, Mo., and will be read with interest, as it fully elucidates what I have already said about the happy family in heaven:

"This great luminary is the central controlling power of our planetary family. The nebulous theory as shown in my previous article is being recognized as the true one, so fast as science is taking the place of bible superstition. Being eternal in the past and to be so in the future, matter has no creator. In one sense, as natural philosophy teaches it is inert, in another it is ever changing. As it had no creator, neither had it any supernatural governor. Its changes and its destination are due to its own inherent nature.

"The sun being in all respects immensely the greatest orb of our solar system, it has excited the more patient and accurate study of astronomers.

"Difficult as this has been, yet much has been learned about it. Its size and distance from us have been measured though, not precisely, still with reasonable certainty. The orbit of our earth being elliptical, we are in parts nearer and again farther from the sun. Hence the average distance is 93,000,000 miles. This distance is too immense to comprehend. By comparisons, however, we try to approximate. The swiftest cannon ball would make the distance in fifteen years. A railroad train at thirty miles per hour would be about 54,000 years in making the trip. A round trip ticket at the usual fare would cost Jay Gould, with his untold millions, more than he could pay. Were a child born of a virgin, fathered by the holy ghost, with arms long enough to reach the sun and silly enough to dip its fingers in it, the inconceivable rapidity of nerve transmission would leave the child more that 100 years without feeling the sensation at its brain.

"The same difficulty confronts us in trying to conceive the size of the sun. Were it hollowed out and our earth dropped in, with its moon 140,000 miles distant circling around us, there would still be space outside left. Its diameter in round numbers is, 852,000 miles; its circumference 2,556,000. At the same time the solid part of the orb is surrounded by its immense photosphere, then a chromosphere, and still a wonderful changing light termed corona.

"While the telescopes, greatly improved in our age of progressive science, have shown much of the surrounding, the last are seen only when the sun is in a total eclipse. For years the most extraordinary efforts have been made by the best astronomers to learn all possible to be seen of these. Nevertheless, the same efforts will continue and photographs be taken of the sun's surroundings. The more visible photosphere and chromosphere yet changing are more easily and accurately examined. The telescope, and more especially the spectroscope, reveal metals in white heat melted to vapor floating in what we may term these atmospheres of the mighty sun. Among them are many of the same nature and constituents of those on our earth. The same is true of the stars, which in all respect are like our sun.

"Again small and great spots of all shapes are seen, and while their locality is not stationary it is enough so to determine the rotary motion of the sun. This is estimated, i. e., its revolution, to be in 28 of our days. The larger spots at times in our clearest atmosphere and with good eyes, may be seen without a magnifier. That they have more or less influence on our planet is about certain. The largest spot yet seen appeared on Nov. 16, 1882, attended by an extraordinary electric storm. Wires and telegrams, as reported by the leading papers of that date, were disastrously disturbed. Astronomers in their patient investigations for the nature and causes of these spots hold varying theories. All agree that they are not solid but of floating gas-like material. The more plausible theory is that they are vast upheavals from a volcanic action of the sun's solid surface, attended as it were by a downheaval of the same matter as it cools and condenses. Some have suggested that the opening allows the sight to go down to the earth's dark surface—but such is not probable.

"The heat continually given out by this great luminary is yet, beyond its distance and size, the more incomprehensible. There is indeed no comparison in each enabling us to grasp or measure the volume of this heat. The heat or fire of all the coal in our world would not keep up the heat radiating from the sun one moment. Millions of meteoric substances, called shooting stars, are constantly descending to our planet. Their qualities and component parts are nearly identical with our own materials. Most of them comparatively small are consumed like matches, lighted by atmospherical friction. The larger ones lodge heated and deeply buried on our surface, and are taken to our museums. Great numbers go to the sun by its greater attraction and contribute to the supply of its heat. And yet, just how it is kept up is an unsolved problem. Its immense downward pressure and condensation explain in part the problem. At the same time there is no reason to doubt its gradual diminution of caloric the chief element concerning us. However as the last lecture I listened to from Procter showed that our earth was losing its surface water to the thickness of a thin sheet of paper annually, so our vast sun parts with no more than that ratio of heat. As in our life time we cannot famish for water, no more may we fear freezing. Certainly not the good family taking my Florida farm at half its value. Besides let us consider that nature is full of adaptation. Animals in or near the frigid zone are thickly furred; in the torrid, naked. **If the elements are to become incapable of sustaining life,** the process will be mild and gradual. So as to the desire of animals to live. A good woman told me years ago that she knew she must soon die, but she still wished to live. So I said you know you must sleep, but now in midday you wish to keep awake. As 9 or 10 o'clock comes you will wish to sleep. And so I said living naturally, will it be as to our final sleep. I stood with her dear children by her side as she sat in her rocker, a month after, she willingly and I may almost add enjoyingly took her last long sleep.

"Nature will take care of her sun, our earth and all its family of planets, with all its sentient beings on them, if we but love and follow here beneficent laws.

"I should have said in connection with the sun's revolution it probably has with its family of planets a greater, grander sweep through the infinite space. Possibly it is destined to get round in trillions upon trillions of years to the same point in its orbit. Yet no finite intellect could more than venture a conjecture. Light travels 12 millions of miles per minute. A star is now seen so far off in space that its light is 3500 years in reaching us. This distance may be less than the diameter of the sun's orbit if he has one. Planets next."

CHAPTER IX.

D URING my pilgrimage I have met many who do not understand what death means. They appear to be so mixed up with the matter of past and present that they are completely muddled.

I will endeavor to clear their minds on that point by references to that which is true and to that which is false.

Death seems to them as the hard words did to the learned schoolmaster of England some two hundred years ago.

Sixty years ago I read John Bunyan's "Pilgrim's Progress" by candle light. In his search after Honesty and Plaindealing John was the positive, but he could not find the two negatives. (Hear! Hear!)

He stumbled upon a very lofty-looking fellow one morning, when the following dialogue occurred:

"Good morning, sir; and can you tell me where the two men I am in search of may be found?"

"What are their names pray?"

"Honesty and Plaindealing."

"No. I know no such beggarly fellows as they.

My conversation is with those of a higher rank."

"Who art thou, pray; and what might be thy rank?"

"I am a school teacher."

"And what do thou teach, pray?"

"I teach hard words, hard sentences, such as manus, domus, and the like."

"Ah! Manus, domus. Pray, what do they mean?"

"They mean manus, domus; and what would you have them to mean else?"

"Yes; but have they no definition?"

"O yes; they define manus and domus and the like."

"Yes, I understand. But have they no signification?"

"Yes, indeed; they signify manus and domus. And what else would you have them to signify?"

And here the pilgrim John failed by the problem of the one positive defining the two negatives, or finding them.

But the reader will remember that that was two hundred years ago.

Don't compare the Johns of two hundred or two thousand years ago with the Johns of to-day.

If the John of here and now does not know more than the John eighteen hundred years ago did, then I am ready to exclaim: "O Christian revelation and progress, in what have you progressed?"

For the information of my readers I will give a brief biographical sketch of the two Johns.

They were both fishermen, without a common school education, but both presumed to teach other men wisdom. But do not be deceived by either of them. Don't believe what they say because they say it. Be men. Dispute every inch of the ground that does not square with your reason.

The first John was born in Capernaum, four furlongs from Tiberus. His father was Zebedee, a fisherman, of Capernaum, who married the daughter of Joseph, a carpenter, of Nazareth in Galilee, by the name of Salome. They had two sons, whose names were James and John. They were brought up as fisher boys, with their father. They were without education. They followed the occupation of fishermen until John was twenty-five years of age. He was born in that obscure town of fishermen 4 years 6 months A. D., and at the age of twenty-five he left that business and became a fisher of men, having a call to catch men instead of fishes as men are caught very much as fish are caught—by deception and force, and in no other way generally.

If the ignorant and perhaps profane and intemperate fishermen were not the proper and best men to promulgate your Christian gospel, then Jesus, whom you call your Lord and Saviour, made a great mistake.

You can take whichever horn of the dilemma you please. I shall be satisfied, and am willing you should enjoy your opinion, but I know whereof I affirm.

I will now give you a short account of the insignificant John whose additional name is Atwood. He was born in that obscure town called Provincetown, fifty-four miles from Boston by water and one hundred and eighteen by land, on December 26, A. D. 1811, at 12.20 p. m., just eighteen minutes after the

81

jury of the apostles had agreed on a verdict that their lord of glory had arisen from the dead, and that time and life were still to go on.

You are aware that doubting Thomas was born on the twenty-first day of December, when the Son of Righteousness had disappeared in the Winter Solstice. He declared that time would be no longer, and that the God of Salvation would never appear again. This story is nothing more nor less than an allegory.

And your John declares in his revelations that he saw the angel of Time standing one foot on the earth and the other foot on the sea, and declared that time should be no longer, and that death and hell were cast into a lake of fire and brimstone, which was the second death.

Now you will perceive that our friend John in his old age had become a little Thomasy and visionary.

Well, John, and his brother fisherman, Peter, that arch deceiver and expert fisherman, had convinced the doubting Thomas.

As I have mentioned this Peter it may be proper to tell who he really was. As there is a large amount of Peterology in the world my readers may want to know where he came from.

Well, as far as we can learn from the account given of him in the New Testament he was the son of Simon a magician of Alexandria, Egypt, and brother of Andrew. They were both ignorant fishermen on the river Niger, and subsequently moved to Capernaum, and sold their fish in the Tiberus market.

This Peter was born in Alexandria, Egypt, seven years before the Christian era. His name was changed when he was called to become a fisher of men.

I forbear giving you his character, but will refer the reader to the writings of his friends in the New Testament. It says indirectly that he was a married man, and that he left his wife and wandered around and had no abiding place, and became so egotistical that I prefer not to say much about him, further than that he killed Ananias and Sapphira, two harmless citizens, for effect as an advertisement for his business, which was catching ignorant men and saving their souls by ticketing them through to heaven, with their baggage checked.

The account given by his friends shows that the evidence of two witnesses, whose character was never impeached, agreed, although given three hours apart; and was overcome by the testimony of one who cursed and swore and lied, and forsook his best friends. Shame on him.

I have charged him with nothing but what his friends say of him.

Now the Jewish law in which they believed, given by Moses, says where two or three witnesses are agreed every word shall be established as truth.

But it makes my heart weary when I see good, well-meaning men, honest in their belief, wandering after what John calls the beast that made fire come down from heaven, as described in the thirteenth chapter of the book of Revelations.

It makes my heart bleed with sympathy for them, but all I can do for them is to show them the true from the false, and let them go on with the erroneous idea of life if they like such a craft and such a voyage; and it is wonderfully strange that full grown men will follow such teachers and believe them to be honest. I have one more John to refer to, and that will fill the list of the John Pilgrims. There are three things to be considered always, and now we have three Johns. The other John was surnamed Bunyan. He wrote an account of his pilgrimage in jail in Bedford, England, while confined there as a criminal.

John the Revelator wrote his pilgrim's progress on the isle of Patmos, having been sent there for having violated the Roman law—it was so decided in court.

Thus you see when they wrote the great works of their lives they were both imprisoned, and both alleged criminals.

They stand in a negative position to me, as I never violated any law of my country, and never have been arrested for any crime. I have commanded thirty-eight different vessels, and have had many differences with officers of the United States, collectors of customs, captains of cutters, and others, but never came off second best.

I never was fined, never smuggled a cent's worth of goods, never wronged the government of the United States nor of the state of Massachusetts to my knowledge, but I have been greatly wronged in my property by both.

I always treated the national and state governments as I did individuals, but I have been robbed by both. I will not advise my readers to deal honestly with either of them. My experience leads me to believe that the present state of affairs will not warrant it, but I advise every man to be honest with himself and other individuals.

I will relate a little of my experience, as it may interest if it does not benefit some of my readers.

I had my vessel, the schooner Ousel of Province-town, wrongly libelled, and I was brought before the United States court. I proved that I had not vio-lated any law, and was acquitted by my plea of self-defence.

I am the only man in the county of Barnstable who ever won his case as an owner of a vessel employed in the codfishery business after having been com-plained of and brought before the United States court, but there have been very many decisions rendered against owners of vessels under bounty law.

Although the case was decided in my favor, I was obliged to pay all the costs of the court. Two years after the decision, and when I was sick in bed, the United States marshal summoned me to appear be-fore the court or pay the costs of one hundred dollars.

I was too ill to appear and told him so, and also that I ought not to be compelled to pay the sum. I objected to signing the bonds because the other party had been exempted. I asked the reason why one should be exempted and not both, and the clerk re-plied that the other was a "sailor man."

I told him I was a "sailor man," and had left my vessel to come to Boston to attend to this case, and that I claimed exemption on the same ground the other party had been exempted. He then told me that I had property while the other man did not have any. Then I replied that there really was less need of my giving bonds, as I could pay costs if I was defeated and would, but he would not reason, and I had to sign. Such is law.

That was some forty years ago, when I was younger than I am now. At that time I supposed there was a disposition in the government officials to deal honestly with the people, but my experience has produced a different opinion concerning some of them at least.

The United States marshal said he knew it was a hard case, and that it was wrong to make me pay the money, but there was no escape from it. He said he had a similar case once on a bark, but they made him pay the costs. I asked him how much the costs of the court were, and he said they were eighty-five dollars, and his fee for coming down and serving the summons was fifteen dollars, making one hundred dollars.

He said he would throw off his fee and five dollars from the court costs, and if the court would not allow it he would pay it out of his own pocket.

I paid the eighty dollars, and thanked him for his kindness, and told him he was a true friend to justice, although he was an officer of the law.

The story of the Good Samaritan, who was a true friend to the suffering man when the priests and deacons of the law passed by on the other side, came vividly to my mind.

I don't ask you to believe this statement, for it may

seem incredible; but I have the papers and can produce them.

There are many other things stranger than fiction which I might relate, but not wishing to be egotistical I forbear.

I always believed more in doing good than in telling others to do so.

CHAPTER X.

THE whole secret concerning life, death and future existence is involved in the misconception as to what really constitutes the soul. The Rev. J. H. Weeks is right when he says the soul is that part of the being which never dies.

I have heretofore explained that that part of man that existed before the individual was formed will exist after the individual has passed away, and is the immortal soul.

But the ego, or I, that is, my thoughts perish at death. What has a beginning must have an ending. But Evolution, Revolution and Dissolution are ever goingon, so the matter which comprises our body, which is the soul, must always move, which is the true nature of our god, who is the god of all the people.

But we have with us a book called the word of another god, which is not in our constitutional Bible to men.

Some of our opponents endeavor to make us believe that the Bible of Moses teaches us the true character of God, while others say that Jesus proves that he is God manifest in the flesh; that is, that man is the omniscient God personified. Thou shalt have no other god besides me, that is man, said Jesus.

This I accept and demonstrate.

But a larger class mix the two contradictory books together, and make hodge-podge of both the Old and New Testaments.

Here I refer to the two separate creations I have pointed out throughout this work.

The last creation is the theological creation. That is the one I am dealing with in this chapter.

If you wish to be wise shut your mouth and open your eyes. You have heretofore been taught the opposite, that is to shut your eyes and open your mouth in order to make you wise. This has been the method followed by your wise teachers. They threw off their manliness, dropped on their knees, shut their eyes, opened their mouths, and prayed to God in the skies.

But we will see what the Book says.

In it we find two accounts of immaculate conceptions. The first was by a male, and the second by a female—both impossible.

The first was alleged to be by the male Lord God, who created Adam of dust, without mixture. That is the definition of the word, and we have no right to dispute the Lord God's word, if we believe him to be the true creator.

Maculate means mixed seed, and is described in the first creation, male and female, every time. Don't get the two stories mixed, because many gods and popular gods have mixed them, and man copied.

The dean of the Divinity School of Harvard University was a level-headed student in theological matters as far as he went, but he did not hew to the line. He feared the chips.

But I must hew to the line if the chips fly in my face. I have no creed but the American, the gospel of which is "the people, by the people, and for the people."

I have no axe to grind; no God to defend or offend. My God is never angry with his offspring. He only carries out his law of life and death inherent in himself without malice or forethought. His fixed law in nature deals alike with all of his children.

I cannot close this chapter better than by adding the remarks of Professor Charles Carroll Everett, dean of the Divinity School of Harvard University, who spoke as follows at a meeting of some two hundred Unitarians at the Hotel Vendome. His subject was "The Person of Christ." He said:

"The present church says that Jesus was God because the older church claimed that he was God.

"I come here to say that he was man.

"Let us look at the circumstances which raised God to the church head. It is not possible to doubt that Jesus was a disciple of John. John baptized him. While the church thought that Christ performed miracles seems to indicate that he was not human, we must remember that other prophets of the Jews performed miracles and were considered human. So, as far as working miracles were concerned, Christ was human.

"Then his resurrection.

"Unquestionably the reappearance of Christ after

death did much to change the minds of the disciples, but even the messiahship of Christ does not prove that he was not human.

"There is no such thing as a mere man, and the question—is God man?—shows which has been at fault. It is not man we want to study, it is God."

CHAPTER XI.

IN this chapter the Evolution theory will be more fully explained, and its truth established, and as it clashes with Hugh Miller's doctrine the latter must be declared to be erroneous.

Mr. Miller makes many assertions, but fails to prove his position.

He says Adam was formed from the dust, and that he received a wife called Eve from his creator, the Lord.

This is mere assertion on his part, but as if to make it more binding he says the men who wrote the records of those days were inspired by the Lord, which is another just as senseless assertion and that it must be true.

That is Mr. Miller's position in opening the affirmative of this discussion.

In behalf of the negative I affirm that I am inspired of God to say that his position is false, and shall so prove it.

He has not offered any tangible evidence to the effect that the first human being was made of full size and of man's stature, instead of passing through the evolution process from infancy to manhood.

As all script or scripture is said to be written by inspiration so am I inspired to write that this earth previous to its formation was simply matter in an indistinguishable mass, or as dust in the air, but by the power of evolution and the force of cohesion a planet was formed, which gravitated to its natural place in the planetary procession, and begun its revolutions around the central planet, or sun, moving as it were a living and intelligent being, although without individual knowledge, but performing its work by force of natural laws which it could not evade.

So the great God formed or evolved all individual beings from this matter, and implanted in them a brain, which, after a healthy development, constituted them beings capable of thinking and acting apparently upon their own responsibility, and held them accountable as such.

(Here ends the theory of Charles Darwin.) And that of John Atwood begins.

Then the creator seemed to say: "Let us form man in our own image, and let him be one of us. And we three be one God, father, son and intelligent spirit in man, male and female; and they shall be fruitful, and multiply and replenish the earth, and have dominion over the earth, and all things thereon."

This finishes our Evolution and Revolution.

So man is the omniscient god, and a part of the great whole, manifested in form.

So is every individual a microcosm, or a little world in himself, but of comparatively short duration on this earth; and when the machine is worn out or disarranged the man ceases to breathe, and then Dissolution performs its part in the programme.

These statements are facts. No matter what we may think or what we may desire, there can be no intelligence without an organized brain, and there can be no brain without material to form it.

All facts are things that exist, and all multiples are but shadows of the facts. The shadow is not anything. The shadow of the most intellectual man who ever lived is without intelligence, and does not even occupy any space.

All religions are founded on dreams, and do not and cannot have any existence in nature.

I have only three books to support my theory of the creation, whereas Hugh Miller has thirty-seven, three-quarters of which are in the Old Testament, but they are contradictory regarding historical facts, dreamy, and disposed to suit the wants of different ages and people.

Job was first placed next to Genesis, being the second book, whereas it is now the eighteenth book in your King James translation of the Bible.

Solomon's Songs, those love stories, were placed in the first chronological account, being the fourteenth book. Now they are the twenty-second book.

I give these as samples of the many changes which have been made, too numerous to record. The names of a great many individuals have also been changed. When bad men became converted to and embraced some particular creed their names were changed, and their old deeds blotted out.

In the New Testament are many such instances, which are acknowledged to be such by the Miller theory, and the work as a whole is no more reliable than is the Old Testament.

True history does not change men's names, nor falsify records. The first collection contained twenty-seven books, whereas King James' translation has only twenty-six, and they are very differently arranged as to position, and many of the dates are merely guessed at. All of which is unsatisfactory from a historical stand point.

Hugh Miller is welcome to his multitude of witnesses who are unable to withstand the searching inquiry of cross-examination.

I will produce only three witnesses, the first being the first chapter of Genesis, giving an account of the creation; the second is the book of Job as originally written, giving man's duty to man; and the third is the unwritten out-door book of nature, the bible of God, ever true and made manifest in the five senses of all human beings.

Those three books are my witnesses, and my opponent has the privilege of cross-examining them as much as he likes. He will find them true at all times.

The sun shines, the wind blows, men are here, and the three make one intelligent life. There could be no intelligence without every one of the three.

My readers must be aware that a monad is an invisible substance without parts. A formal atom or atoms combined, like a mass of water, show life when acted upon by the wind; but when it is unmoved and the sun shines upon it, it stagnates or dies, as it is termed, but really is passing through a change and forms another and different organic body, which is still at the work of Evolution, creating as it were millions of living individuals that can fly in the air.

They are formed without paternal transmission, and have neither father nor mother, nor do they ever produce offspring, no children, nor grandchildren; but they make themselves known when their sting enters our flesh. We know they are there.

The mosquito does not produce its like, as do other animals, but are full grown when they launch forth, like Hugh Miller's Adam; but they are not formed out of dust.

Dust is death without liquid, and cannot be made into a living body by God or man without a mixture. Water is life itself, and when a mass dies it forms a living being, without or with dust, as the case may be in the formation of larger beings, but all of them are maculate productions.

CHAPTER XII.

SECTARIANISM is a fearful thing in our midst. It is stealing silently along in the dark like a midnight assassin, with a drawn dagger, and will plunge it deep in the heart of the nation if not checked.

The first Christian church organized, and which laid claim to being the only Christian church, you admit has the prior claim to Christianity. This is indisputable. There is a larger proportion of criminals in that church than in any other, or among infidels and atheists. They furnish a less number of criminals in proportion to their numbers than any Christian sect.

So much for pure Christianity, if there is any.

But we should be thankful that the Bible furnishes so many ways to get to heaven, and sets those pious people quarrelling, or we should be all lost, and not one of us would dare say our soul was our own.

My friends know, or ought to know, that our government is based on the right of the people to govern, and that the people own the land and property comprised within the United States, and when any one sect secures a majority that sect will set up a monarchy and declare Jesus the King and ruler of the nation, as Massachusetts did under the reign of our good Puritans. In open violation of the United States constitution they declared State sovereignty and put King Jesus at the head.

Their governor was only commander-in-chief over the military forces, but the ministers of Jesus had to be supported by the State. All children were born orthodox, and when they arrived at the age of sixteen all males had to pay a tax to that church, whether their parents attended worship there or not.

My father and mother were Methodists and members of a church of that denomination. My grandfather and great-grandfather were Methodists.

But I was born Orthodox, and should have had to certificate over to the Methodists at the age of sixteen as my older brother had done, but the law was modified before I arrived at that age.

I will relate a little story of my great-uncle, which occurred soon after the war of 1812. He was taken a prisoner by the English, but in a short time was given his liberty. He was very poor and in critical circumstances. To use his own words, which he printed in a book about 1827, the tithes gatherer threatened to levy on his property for what he called the support of the gospel, and decided to take his cow.

Winter was approaching, and to look at the wan features and emaciated forms of his wife and two young children was like driving daggers to his heart.

This he says led him to search the Bible to see what the gospel of Christ was, and he found it purported to be glad tidings unto all of the people; but he had learned from experience that a law said to be established by authority of the gospel was sad tidings of great grief to many men.

I write this because many of my readers will hardly believe that our good old Orthodox fathers were so good as to give God all the glory, and a right to all the land and property besides. They declared that the earth was the Lord's and the fulness thereof, and some contend for that now.

Happy mortals! They don't own a foot of the land they stand on, and do not dare to say that their souls are their own.

I was unfortunate in being born where I was and when I was, as the rulers of our government and our State say I was born a squatter; and my father and grandfather were born squatters, and so were all the people now living in Provincetown who were born there. So says the lighthouse board at Washington. I have letters from them to that effect.

I quote Lyman Abbott, the great Orthodox leader. He is fifty years ahead of Beecher's time. I have no need of quoting him to prove what I say of Bible teaching. He is opening his eyes to historical facts.

But I must tell you a little about the ownership of Massachusetts. The teachers called of God to proclaim His ownership declared that they were right, and quoted the word of God, as they called it.

They declared that Nebuchadnezzar, the King of the Chaldeans, was driven from his kingly throne into the fields, on his hands and knees, like a beast, and made to eat grass, or straw, like an ox, and be wet with the dews of the night from heaven, until he knew that the most high God ruled the affairs of men and appointed over them whomsoever He would (this is Israelitish fraud). Clouds of ignorance.

Consult your Bible, and you will find that God or gods gave to man the whole creation, and he was to have dominion over the earth and every thing therein. Dominion is ownership or possession, and Nebuchadnezzar was right in claiming the property; but the upstart Jewish rabbis claimed everything for their Lord God, and the ministers of Massachusetts claimed it for the word of God to frighten men and women into obedience, and they did it for a while.

But I can hardly believe they were such fools as to believe it. It was done to frighten the people (as I have said) on the same principle that parents relate to their children the Elisha bear story, that is, to scare them into staying in the house on the Sabbath.

I believe they did it as a scarecrow to keep their children in so they could not play out of doors. Some of them might have been sincere.

I was taught by my father and mother that two she bears came out of the woods and tore forty and two children in pieces because they said to an old man: "Go up, bald head." I have no doubt that they believed the story, but that don't make it so. They told me I must not go out of doors on Sunday, and if I did the bears would come out of the woods and carry me off.

This was done to scare me, for they knew there were not any bears in our woods, and the further and more substantial fact was that there were no woods, let alone there being any bears.

Dr. Abbott made another great mistake when he said that Paul showed his faith by his works. (I deny it.) He taught that by grace are ye saved, and not by works, lest any man should boast. And again, "if through my lie the grace of God doth more abundantly abound," why is it computed to me as sin? (that is the lie).

Paul taught that salvation depended wholly on the faith that Jesus was the Christ, and had risen from the dead.

It was the bishop at Jerusalem, called James the Just, the son of Alpheus and the other Mary, who was the Lord's brother after the flesh, that is he was half brother to Jesus, they having one father but two mothers. James believed in good works, rather than faith, he says, to others. Show me your faith without works and I will show you my faith with works.

James did not believe that Jesus arose from the grave, and did not preach it at Jerusalem. He was appointed to preach to the Jews by the other Apostles in that great city, and was murdered by Paul before Paul was converted to the Thereputian doctrine; and now he and his friends steal James' thunder and claim that it was written to the Hebrews from Italy by Timothy. But it is not true.

James wrote this epistle to the Hebrews when Paul was Saul, the bad boy. And a bad fellow he was then, just the stuff they make saints of.

CHAPTER XIII.

THIS chapter will contain much information for the fishermen and business men of Cape Cod generally. Look out for your interests, or you will lose what I have gained for you. I have been informed that the Old Colony is delaying freight to your disadvantage.

The following is a list of freight rates from Provincetown to Boston from 1876 to 1882. In 1877, under the old rates, $1.00 per box billed at 500 pounds; 50 cents per barrel billed at 250 pounds. The same rates for fast or slow freight.

In 1878 the rates were the same on boxes or barrels without regard to their weight. There was a slight increase in business from the previous year.

In 1879 the rates were the same until the last part of the season, when the Old Colony railroad company doubled the rates on the morning train, which brought the most of the fish because the slow or regular freight was so long on the road that it did not pay to ship by that train, as fish put on board the train Thursday afternoon would not arrive in Boston Friday in season to be sold that day, and hence on Saturday morning the fish would be in poor order and the sale of the week over.

Therefore it became necessary to send by the train that left Friday morning, about 5 o'clock, arriving in Boston about 10.20 the same day.

The same fish leaving Provincetown Thursday evening would be switched off at Yarmouth or some other station, and attached to the morning train and taken through and received at Comercial wharf from 11.30 to 12.30, or as soon as they could be got at, our teamsters unloading the cars by permission of the freight agent or clerks, in order to expedite business.

But as business had increased under this arrangement the Old Colony railroad thought proper to double up the rates, although then we were having to pay more than double the rates from Portland by either of her roads.

I saw that our trade in cod and haddock would be spoiled, as we could not compete with Portland, nor could we pay so high freight, in many instances amounting to five times as much as the Boston and Maine or the Eastern road charged.

Therefore I wrote to Mr. Choate, the president of the Old Colony road, saying to him that if he thought the freight from Provincetown was worth looking after I would like to have an interview with him at any place he might select.

I received from him a reply appointing a time, and the place his office. He called in Mr. Kendrick, the general passenger agent, and Mr. Putnam, the general freight agent.

I produced my bills and sustained the charges I

had made, viz., that they were charging five times as much as other roads. I presented a bill from Provincetown for thirteen boxes and one barrel, for which we had paid $34.00.

I showed them one received the same week from Portland for twenty boxes for which we paid $10.00, it being for the same kind of fish and the same size of boxes, called long boxes, containing about 500 pounds of fish, say 600 pounds gross.

The difference per box was $2.10, which was more than the profit could have been, and it would not need a prophet to tell what would be our fate.

I urged that they do something to save the business over their road, for in so doing our business would be saved; but it was useless.

I further said that if I was at Provincetown I would put on a line of vessels and run the fish to Boston, as I had done before; but I did not know what the shippers would do, as they were somewhat at variance. They did not do anything, and the business was ruined in less than two years.

So the business of Atwood & Co. was nearly ruined by exorbitant freight rates and slow transit. The estimates of the injury which we received from those causes have been placed from eight to ten thousand dollars in the three years.

The producers and shippers of the Cape lost the opportunity of making a good many thousand dollars. and the Old Colony suffered largely on that account.

A rate of one dollar per box for transporting the fish would have yielded more profit to the company that $2.00 to $2.60, as that was nearly prohibitory, and greatly reduced the volume of business done by the road.

I know what the general freight agent said was the reason why they put the freight on that train, but as I have no witnesses I think it prudent not to mention it here.

At a subsequent time, however, in the presence of witnesses, he gave another reason, which I valued very much.

It was before the Railroad Commissioners, when I was contending for a night train and lower rates.

Through our exertions and the suggestions and decisions of the Honorable Judge Russell, together with the Board of Railroad Commissioners, the Old Colony Railroad Company granted our request and put on a night freight train, which has been the means through which Cape Cod people have received a good many thousands of dollars more than they would have received under the arrangement of 1883.

Therefore we feel satisfied on that point. It has been a good thing for Cape Cod producers and shippers, and they were well satisfied except in the matter of unequal charges for freight, some paying from ten to fifty per cent. more than others, the lowest price having been made for the longest distance.

We received many complaints and letters soliciting us to remedy this. Of course we knew who paid the highest and who paid the lowest, as we received fish from more than one hundred shippers over the Old Colony road. We applied for an equalization of rates by the urgent request of some of our patrons.

We had two hearings before the railroad commissioners, but they decided in favor of the corporation.

The counsel for the company set up the plea that they had a right to charge what they pleased. Their depot masters would borrow scales and weigh a few packages and guess at the rest about all the season. In many instances they charged too much, but very seldom too little.

We had the means of knowing whether the right weight was charged on the way bill or not. I suppose the gentleman set up his claim by the construction of chapter 225, acts of 1882, as there is no other statute law which in my opinion could be construed to justifiy such a claim.

The two words "undue" and "unreasonable" do not come within my comprehension of the law. Therefore, I say, away with such outlandish terms

Laws ought to be made so they can be understood by lawyers, if not by the people.

I did not refer to either of the acts of 1882, for the reason that I was really ashamed of the last act, which was supposed to take the precedence; and I suppose the Honorable Judge Russell looked at it in that light, as he made no mention of either of the acts, but referred to section 190 of chapter 112, acts of 1874, every time he mentioned the statute laws.

I must say I cannot agree with him in his decision, and think that section is somewhat complicated; but how he could draw such conclusions from it is more than I can understand.

Chapter 94 of 1882 is so plain that a man might

run and read and understand. That is what the people want.

But it is policy for lawyers to have it otherwise.

I am for the people's rights, every time.

Chapter 225 was not mentioned by the commissioners. It was the last act, and ought to have had the preference, had it been legal.

I will tell you why. It was because it was used as a dark horse by the corporations to ride over the people, and Judge Russell must have considered it so, or he would have referred to it, because the judge knew that section 190 of chapter 112, acts of 1874, had been superseded by chapter 94 of the acts of 1882; hence it was null and void as far as it related to discrimination in freight rates. Therefore his decision on discrimination in the case of John Atwood versus the Old Colony Railroad Company has no warrant or standing in law, and the railroad commissioners must know it as well as I do.

This was his excellency's decision in his inaugural address. He sustained my position. The whole scheme must have been concocted to deceive the people, for I hardly am prepared to say that any lawyer of Boston will contend that a dead letter law, or one that has been covered over by two subsequent acts, is still in force.

Section 190 of chapter 112 is not as good as a last year's almanac as far as discrimination in freight rates is concerned.

Let them face the music, and not go into antiquity and dig up sections of skeleton laws instead of using living ones.

If the legislators of 1882, who made two laws on the subject, one perfect, and honored the previous law with a fixed penalty, and subsequently made another which did not honor the previous law, and had no penalty affixed and was not definite—then, I ask, which could supersede (a query).

It is all seen clearly by the eye of psychometry, by which I know all things I state to be true.

I have in my possession two letters written to me previous to this contention by Judge Russell in answer to a question as to what constitutes discrimination on freight rates.

The answer in both letters was just what I proved against the Old Colony Railroad Company before him, but he decided against his own knowledge and against his own decision, doubly given to me over his own signature.

His motive for so doing I leave with you to decide.

O, Almighty Dollar, what is there thou canst not do?

We read in that sacred book from the best authority, if there is any difference in that respect, "Thou art not thy own, but thou art bought with a price."

That's a fact.

I realize in my experience that every man has a price for his honesty and integrity.

A very small price will buy some men.

CHAPTER XIV.

DANIEL gives you a dreamy account of Babylon and its kings, but it is not reliable. He takes a very round about way to do it, and relates many foolish dreams about all the beasts we can think of. He tells of their horns, great horns having little horns which were transformed into kings, and other such crazy dreams called the word of God in the Bible Creation, which I do not acknowledge.

I will give you a few quotations, but I want you to read the whole book of Daniel as you would any other book, and then consider what a reliable witnes you have.

He says of King Nebuchadnezzar that he was driven from men and ate grass as oxen, and his body was wet with the dew of heaven, till his hairs were grown like eagles' feathers, and his nails like birds' claws, that he might know the Most High God ruleth in the kingdom of men and giveth it to whomsoever he will.

Now God or gods had given everything to man long before Daniel's day, and Daniel makes his Lord God take the dominion that the gods gave unto the

109

Chaldeans, but this story was made to order, so it could end as the writer wished like a novel.

Now Daniel speaks of Belshazzar and says that he, Daniel, was namedby the king Beltishazzar. Who ever saw such foolish egotism. The idea that a great king of Babylon would call a wandering Jew slave for a Chaldean nobleman is so preposterous that it is silly if man was the author.

But all through the Bible record names must be changed. All liars, thieves, murderers and wicked men have made a practice of changing their names from the time of Adam even until now.

Well, we will give you a little more of Daniel and his story of the three Hebrew worthies, Shadrach, Meshack and Abednego, who were cast into the fiery furnace and came out unscorched, not even the smell of fire about their garments. (Wonderful.)

And there is Daniel himself who was cast into the den of hungry lions, and after being there all night was not even scratched. (Wonderful, wonderful.)

What a tremendous smart fellow this Daniel was. But it was all a dream.

I wrote you about my brother fisherman, John, that good boy, and that the book of Revelations written by him was a Hebrew book, and not a Christian book, and that John had left them because he was ill-treated, and wrote the book of Revelations, condemning them all except the few interpretations that served to make it excel except as a New Testament book. As John had been one of them they could not afford to lose him.

But I stated that the book was a book of the Old

Testament, as it gave internal evidence of that fact. But I will give you more evidence. It is almost an exact copy of part of the book of Daniel, and was copied from that book of dreams, and submitted to the seven synagagues in Asia, called Christian churches, but were not. Six hundred and sixty-six persons could not run seven churches.

I know I repeat these sayings and references several times in my book, but you have been so long taught wrong in regard to Bible teachings that you require to have it forcibly impressed upon you.

I have impressions which were made upon my mind when I was young that I know are wrong, but they frequently appear to me now.

CHAPTER XV.

THERE are two through tracks to heaven. If my readers will go with me through this chapter I will introduce to them some of the theologies of the past and present, and demonstrate to them by the rule of three who the authors were and are.

The theologies are many in branches, but I shall name only three, which will cover all the ground.

And by the rule of trigonometry, the one true and positive part, I shall take the affirmative, and prove the two negatives untrue.

This is not the common nor acknowledged form of discussion to-day. One affirmative and one negative is the order; but I believe in progression, and that truth in the future must prevail. We must have three parts to make a square.

The indication is that the time is coming when men will know more and be better than they are to-day, although to-day it is a great improvement upon the past, when false theology reigned triumphant.

The question is: Resolved, That man's love for man is the best religion of this age; and I John take the affirmative and introduce to my readers Abou Ben Adhem, the lover of his fellow-man.

When the angel of the Lord came around to see where the best man could be found, Abou asked the angel what he was searching for, and the angel replied that he sought those who loved the Lord. Abou then inquired if his name was on the records as such, and when told that it was not he said to the angel, "then write me down as one who loves my fellow-man."

Subsequently the angel came around to reward the blessed, when it was discovered that Abou Ben Adhems's name led all the rest.

This I term Abou Ben Adhemology, positive good.

My opponents are two in this discussion, and they both claim the love of man toward God to be paramount to all others, but we will see at the close of this discussion which of them will triumph.

The two theologies by name are Peterology and Paulology, because they were the founders. And here I give their doctrines as they proclaimed and taught and defended them.

First, Peterology in as shellbark, with very little meat, mostly shell, like a school book (so it seems to me).

Peter declared that he held the keys of the kingdom of heaven, which were intrusted to his care, and that he was the only person who could open the door and admit or reject whomsoever he pleased, and that he had a right to appoint his successor and give him the keys; so the popes in succession are his vice-regents, and they can appoint whomsoever they will, and give them authority to ticket on a through train to heaven and check their baggage all who will take their road and pay for the ticket. So if they go on a through train they are sure, and no freight train allowed on that track, which might wreck it.

But stop there, says my other opponent. As Elihu said to Job and his friends, I have a word to say, too.

Paul comes and takes the floor and says: "I have another track laid through to heaven, with palace and sleeping cars, with every convenience, and will ticket you through without money and without price. I give you a free pass, but you must risk your baggage, if you have any; but it is not necessary for you to take any, as we provide you with everything you will need or can make use of on your passage.

"I, Paul, say that the other road is a humbug, and gotten up to extort money from the poor; and as your Great Teacher said, the poor you always have with you, but I am not always with you; he has delegated this doctrine to me, and so I delegate it to you, my followers. As I said to the Corinthians, so I say unto to you, the gospel of our Lord is free. Did I take anything of you for my services? Did Timothy, my son, charge anything for his services? Free gospel.

"And now I declare unto you if any other man preaches unto you any other doctrine than I have declared unto you, let him be accursed. (That is, curse him.) Yea, if an angel come from heaven and preach to you any other doctrine save that I have preached, let him be accursed." (That is, curse him.)

This seemed to be a settler for my first opponent, and I could sit and laugh to myself to see those two eat

114

themselves as the famed Kilkenny cats did in the allegory.

But in this discussion my last opponent got the largest vote and was declared the winner later on.

So I have now but one negative on the question. The first opponent claims the right to the floor, but he has been ruled out by an overwhelming vote.

So I shall leave the Peterite, and attack the Paulology, and with the aid of my learned and wise and able friend, Joe Howard, the wise and good man, the writer of his love for man in the Sunday Globe, a man who tells the truth and shames the devil at all times and on all subjects. And no man dares or thinks himself able to oppose him. I know of no one who has had the determenation to do it.

So my colleague in this discussion stands head and shoulders above every other writer on truth, humanity and the realization of this life.

So I introduce to you Mr. Howard of the Sunday Globe, who takes his motto from David, Paul's great idol, whom he terms a man after God's own heart, and says of that God: "In my anger I said that all men are liars." (I wish to qualify this before Mr. Howard opens. I presume that David meant that all men who proclaimed that there was a personal God outside of man were liars. So be it. So be it.)

Now, this discussion will be finished with a few closing remarks by the opener.

I am well acquainted with Paul, that is by what he says of himself and what his friends say of him.

He has declared some truths, which have been referred to in this work. And I am well acquainted with many of his followers, and very excellent men some of them are, too. I would unhesitatingly believe them when they speak concerning anything that is knowable; but when they take wings as Paul did and fly off into space, looking for unknown gods—as Paul did to the Athenians at the great Aripagos at Mars Hill—then I let them go as the wise Athenians did Paul, as he seemed to like the voyage.

But now I take leave of Paul for a time and pay my respects to some of his followers.

The great Spurgeon of England said in one of his sermons: "I have always considered that Jesus took the cup of wine in both of his hands, after the manner of the east and at one tremendous draught drank damnation dry."

But I will come nearer home, so that you can verify my statements. I will quote from what Sam Jones called a sermon which he delivered in Boston. He took his text from, and a very unsavory text it was. It was from Paul's writings, and in his efforts to explain it he showed that he was as ignorant of it and of the character of the author as I am of the writings of Bob Dignay in his book called "Lalepilia," and I never read a word of it.

His text was the thorn in Paul's flesh. He handled it seemingly as clumsily as a cow would handle a musket. I will not judge him and say he was a fool or a knave, but I will give you what he said in part as reported in the Boston papers, and leave you to judge. I will not give his argument in full, but will say it was foreign to the subject.

116

In the course of his remarks he stopped suddenly and said: "I suppose you think I talk foolishly, but you must remember that it is a foolish audience that I am talking to." This being a sample you can judge what the rest must have been.

Perhaps it was true when applied to a part of his audience, for those who left their business, spent their time and money on Sam Jones, and listened to his vain babbling I think would fill the bill.

But it seems to be the disposition of many to give credence to all that a reformed drunkard, who was picked up from the gutter, as he says he was, may say, and there is a class of persons who hug such men to their bosoms.

Well, it may accord with their religion, but our folks don't like it. It is in keeping with Watts and Edwards. Dr. Watts says that while the lamp holds out to burn the vilest sinner may return. And some of the apostles declared that there was more joy in heaven over one sinner who repents than over ninety and nine just persons who need no repentance.

That is giving a license to do wrong and then repent; take the benefit of the act, and escape all punishment; and then have ninety-nine honors to a good man's one. I say such preaching is disgusting to any good, honest, square kind of a man,

I can see the reason why most of the convicts in our prisons are believers in this doctrine, and well they might be, as it ensures them such great profits from such investments, and figure largely on the laws of there being such great reward for their wickedness, as there are plenty of priests ready to administer the unction and give them a ticket through to heaven. They make a speech on the scaffold before they are hanged, and then are swung off into heaven, where they are told will be great rejoicing.

This is horrible in a country like ours, where its constitution locates its heaven here and now, and good men are its occupants, and the best men of the country have the most honors, or ought to have.

This false Peter and Paulology fills our prisons and asylums to overflowing, and is largely the cause that fills the suicide's grave.

It is time that the voters of this beloved country should wake up and see their danger, and put their foot on the monster serpent whose fangs are bare, ready to sap the life blood of the nation. Treason in its worst form is allowed to stalk abroad.

I know there are a few good men, true to their friends, who differ from them. They are true to every one and honest at heart, and I love them as men. But as they belong to a party they can't be true to themselves in an emergency and be sound on the goose, which means go for your party and church, right or wrong, and have no scruples about what is right or wrong here, individually.

I hope the rulers of this country will see their danger, and take warning, and realize that they live in the nineteenth century, and profit by the small Christian republics, and see that they fulfil the prophecies given in the New Testament. I am sorry to wound the feelings of my good friends, but the necessity is laid on me, and woe is me if I stifle the truth.

The crisis is approaching. I shudder to think of

it. The truth that Jesus is said to have declared is being fulfilled. " I come not to bring peace, but the sword, and to set father against son, and son against father; mother against daughter, and daughter against mother, etc., etc." It is being fulfilled, in part, every day.

O horrible, horrible. Horum, Croum, Planetorum, Plenevento.

The people are deceived. Deceived let them be. This is the ancient priests' motto.

But I say unto the American people that we have in our constitution no visionary heaven or hell.

And let us declare that all those who have made an agreement with hell in the distance to frighten the negative of our people to follow them that their agreement shall not stand in our free government of the people, by the people, and for the people.

CHAPTER XVI

BEGINNING with the second chapter of Genesis, or the generation of the heavens, we find a new heaven and a new earth, by an entire new author. He testifies for himself, as follows:

What is your name?

Lord God.

Where do you dwell?

In the heavens.

Did you create or make this earth and the heavens out of nothing?

Yes.

Did you plant a garden in the eastern part of Eden?

Yes.

Did you form man out of the dust of the ground and breathe into his nostrils the breath of life, and he became a living being, or soul?

Yes.

Was he a dead soul before your breath was put into him?

Yes.

Did you make man before you made vegetable or animal life?

Yes.

Did you make man of the male gender, and demand that he should, while alone, name all the plants, birds, fishes, and every species of animal before you created or made a woman for him?

Yes.

Did you tell the man after he had been operated upon, and a rib taken from him, that he had the liberty to eat from every tree in the garden except one?

Yes, I did.

What was your object in keeping man more ignorant than the beasts of the field, birds of the air, or fishes of the sea? They all know good from bad.

I was afraid that if man could know good from evil, he, being in our image, would rebel, and there would be war in heaven, and it proved to be so, as is recorded in my book of Revelations.

Did you make the serpent?

Yes.

Don't you perceive that the serpent outwitted you and carried the day, and that Mother Eve and Father Adam are as young to-day as they ever were; and instead of being the fruit of death it became the tree of life?

Well, I dont see it in that light.

You are stuck, and Satan has the best of the argument this time. Why did you deliver two of your children, Philetus and Hymenæus, over to Satan, that he might teach them not to blaspheme? Were you incompetent, or was the devil a better teacher for your children than you were.

You make me angry. I will leave you.

But stop. Be not indignant. I have a few more questions to ask.

Go on. I have no time to answer wicked men's questions.

Do you call me wicked because you cannot answer my questions? Did the men and women really hide from you so you could not find them without halloaing for them? How could you be omnipresent and not know who told them that they were naked? Was Cain born a wicked man because his mother ate the sweet apple, and did you make Adam full grown at first, or did he grow up like other men?

Then came this indignant reply: "O foolish man, what are you talking about? I go. I am the Lord God."

Well, good-by. I may meet you again, when I shall have other questions to propound.

* * * * * * * *

Good morning, Mr. Lord God, if thou art not in anger.

Did you not curse the serpent because he beguiled the woman?

Yes.

Did the offence cause the woman to have children?

Yes.

Did Eve bring forth Cain because of this wicked act?

Yes.

Did you quit gardening and throw the labor on

122

Adam, and make him sweat for a living because those parents were to have a family of children? Don't you perceive that that is the only way to keep the world populated? And your predecessor, the first creator, God (or gods), made all animate nature, male and female, and commanded them to multiply and replenish the earth. Did you want to live alone and make fools of Adam and Eve?

I won't answer any of your questions.

Don't get angry. Good day.

I will ask some of your prophets and inspired wise men concerning your acts towards your people. And then I will see if you continue in anger as I left you. Good-by. I shall challenge and cross-examine your witnesses as I think proper.

*   *   *   *   *   *   *   *

I find the following quotation of scripture ready-made in Gore's "Rambler," with the prefix god or lord every time. This god, meaning the Israelitish Lord God and not the Chaldeans' God mentioned in the light of reason while you are in running order and harmonize with that ever-present but invisible God and his sun.

Now don't accuse me of stealing your God. I have not done it, unless you worship a phantom for a god, and if you do let him go; he is not worth keeping. I would not harm you, dear reader, and if you are wedded to your idol, go on. I am satisfied after I have done my duty as a brother.

Ephraim can have his own way and worship strange gods if he likes.

Here I append what the true birth should be, as given to the ladies of Boston, Dr. Landis said.

The clippings I give you are such as wise men give to their hearers, but you must not think it is all wisdom. You will remember that Satan was the wise god, fully versed in the art of deception in the second creation.

I submit a few questions for thinkers:

Can any man be so foolish as to believe that there is a personal god outside of man and animals, with wisdom enough to discern good from evil?

There is but one reasonable conclusion to come to, and that is the one that Elder Snowball came to, that when God directed Rabbi Helchiah to pen the second creation as you have it he did not think that there would be any man fool enough to believe it true. There was the quail story, the dry dust story, the Jonah story, in fact all the crooked stories in the six books invented by that wicked Rabbi, aided by that arch lawyer, Phefan, making men live nearly a thousand years, so as to date their record ahead of other nations.

I wonder that we find men to-day dabbling in such silly stuff, but it has become the order of the day. And a man is considered a simple ignoramus or a wicked sinner if he don't conform to some one of those side issues; and if he does he has a few squeezed up ones within him, and thousands of strong able-bodied men against him. A house divided against itself shall not stand, nor an agreement with hell avail them anything.

* * * * * * * *

I submit the following clippings for thinkers:

Would endless punishment be for the good of any human being?

If God loves his enemies, will he punish them any more than is for their good?

If God loves his friends, if he loves his enemies also, is not mankind an object of his love?

If God loves only those who love him, what better is he than any sinner?

As "love thinketh no evil," can God design the ultimate evil of a single soul?

If man does wrong in returning evil for evil would not God do wrong in doing the same thing?

Would not endless punishment be a return of evil for good?

If God hates the sinner, would it not be natural for the sinner to hate him?

If God loves his enemis now, will he not always love them?

Would it be unjust in God to be kind to all men in a future state?

If all men deserve endless punishment, will not those who are saved miss divine justice?

Does divine justice require the infliction of pain from which mercy recoils?

If God would save all men but cannot, is he infinite in his power?

If God can save all men and will not, is he infinite in his goodness?

Did God desire universal salvation when he created men?

Will God carry his orignal designs into execution?

Can God will anything contrary to his knowledge?

Did God know when he created man that a large portion of his creatures would be endlessly wretched?

If he did not know all at the creation is he infinite in knowledge?

If God made an endless hell, did he do so for the express purpose of burning men in it?

If an angel be born a devil by sinning was Adam's the original sin?

Would there be any more impropriety in imputing my sin to Adam than his to me?

If men are totally depraved must not children be also?

If children are totally depraved, how is it true "that of such is the kingdom of heaven?"

Is it the revealed will of God that all men should be saved?

Could God will that all men should be saved when he knew that many would be lost?

If belief and good works are essential to salvation, how can infants be saved?

Can he truly love God who worships him through fear of the devil?

Can the love of God be changed to hatred?

Can the Deity be universally good, if endless pun_ ishment is meted out to a single soul?

Can good men worship a being who has created millions for endless torture?

Are those not the enemies of God who charge such conduct upon him?

Can it be virture to charge a good being with the most abominable characteristics?

If God made all things and knew all things ; if he made the Devil, knowing he would lead mankind astray, will it be just to punish mankind for it ?

Would not a being who would do this be as bad or worse than the Devil?

If the Devil is the author of endless hell fire, would it not be the noblest thing God could do to put it out ?

If God created an endless hell before he created man, did he know there would be any use for it ?

If God knew there would be any use for an endless hell, must he have not created some men for endless misery ?

If God created an endless hell, was it included in the works he pronounced " very good?"

If there be an endless hell, and it was not made before creation, when was it made ?

If there be a personal Devil, who made him, and for what purpose was he made ?

Can there be any such thing as sin in heaven ?

If there was sin in heaven, and angels were cast out, may there not be sin in heaven again, and the present inhabitants be cast out ?

As sin possesses temptation of some sort, who tempted a holy angel to sin?

If an angel could sin without a Devil to tempt him, may we not sin without a Devil to tempt us ?

If a holy angel was tempted by surrounding evil, is heaven a holy place ?

If an angel was tempted by evil passions could he have been holy ?

* * * * * * * *

127

According to the records there were men who as
pedestrians walked longer than any man can walk
now. Enoch walked with the Lord three hundred
years, got beat and died; and God buried him (but
did not put a tablet or monument at his grave, or
even stick up a piece of board at his grave so that
his friends could find the body). So says Helchiah,
the Jewish rabbi, aided by Phefan, the scribe or
lawyer.

He got the first six books accepted as the word of
God by that blessed youth who loved the Lord and
sought the truth (King Josiah, a boy, eight years old),
five books ascribed to Moses, one to Joshua. He wrote
an account of his own death, but no evidence was
given that his writings were true. Moses also wrote
of his own death.

Hence they stand with Joseph Smith's fifteen books
of Mormon. I have read them thoroughly, and they
don't compare in reason with "Gulliver's Travels,"
the "Arabian Nights' Entertainments," "Baron Mun-
chausen's Tales," or Mark Twain's book, "Roughing
It."

Making men to live nearly a thousand years was a
shrewd trick to place the early records of the Israelites ahead of their time and give them great
antiquity.

CHAPTER XVII.

THAT Christianity originated in Egypt about the
year A. D. 1 there can be no reasonable doubt,
and that the monks of Alexandria were the propa-
gators is plain to be seen, and they were not called
Christians until near the end of the first century.

They were first called Christians at Antioch by
Theophilus Ignatius, the fanatic, a writer of many
books of the New Testament and a large writer of
the Apocraphy of the New Testament.

Philo was a teacher in one department of that
great school at Alexandria, and taught what he called
the contemplative life, and had for his pupils
Jesus of Nazareth and Judas of Tiberus in Galilee.

You will find those boys connected somewhat in
their youth, as given in the Apocraphy of the New
Testament by Ignatius, as I have copied from that
book. In it Judas is called the bad boy, but I will
let you decide which the bad boy is according to the
records given.

After they had finished their education Judas went
to Tiberus and formed a new sect, called the smaller
sect, of the Essenes, and drew many after him ; and

Jesus came and dwelt in Capernaum, four furlongs from Tiberus. They joined hands in this social doctrine, and Judas was to carry the bag of money, and they were to have all things in common.

In regard to the future life they both taught the resurrection of the human body, but subsequently they disagreed and quarrelled about it, as Paul and Barnabas did about letting the old man John go to see his friends.

Jesus proclaimed that the Jews would destroy the temple of his body and God would raise it up again in three days; but Judas disputed it, and said by way of evidence that bodies had been embalmed by the thousands for more than a thousand years, and not one had been raised, and never would be until the resurrection day, which would be at the closing of human life on this earth, which was to be at the ending of that generation; and if their policy could have been carried out and no children had been born after that generation the first part of the prophecy would have been fulfilled more than a thousand years ago.

But the raising of all those dead bodies would have been another matter over which the priests could have had no control. Although they had promised them another individual life, they would never get it.

For the truth of what I have written look into your Bible, and read what Jesus says at the supper table. He says: "You twelve have I chosen, and one of you hath a devil (that is, he opposes me)." That made Peter nervous, and he asked: "Who is it?" and Jesus replied: "He that dips sop with me in the same dish shall betray me."

Then Judas threw down the bag of money and left the clan of Apostles and never associated with them again.

This was no betrayal. It was Peter who betrayed his Master when he was set as a watch to look out for their enemies, the Jews, as they had disobeyed the Jewish laws, and if caught he would be crucified. That they knew.

But Peter, that sleepy fisherman, would not keep awake, not even one hour, nor keep his men awake when danger was so nigh. Shame on him! It was the worst act I ever knew a fisherman to do And than he ran off after betraying his Master by his negligence and denied him, and cursed and swore and lied, and said he did not know him. (Outrageous.)

He was a pretty fellow to establish the Christian church on and give the keys of the kingdom of heaven to, and let him shut out whomsoever he pleased.

Verily! Verily! Verily! The New Testament is a wonder. I am giving you a sketch of the early authors of what is called Christianity, but Christianity to-day is different. It is claimed to be justice, goodness and virtue. If those be its attributes they had better drop such characters as the founders of Christianity were, and be good on their own merits and not depend on Jesus, Peter and Paul for their salvation.

I think this is enough to show the origin of Christianity.

And now for the establishment and promulgators of it. It was established in Rome, in the year 312 of the Christian era by that wicked emperor, Constantine,

131

who abolished paganism and established Christianity, and set himself up as the first pope successor to Peter.

Some writers say he called a convention at Nice, in the province of Bothnia, in 325 ; but others say it was in 327, which I think was the more probable, as he had the queen's mother put to death in 325, his own son, 326 A. D. He was a slayer of men, women and children.

The Nicene synod was called to prefer a charge of heresy against one Ariast who had dissented from the true faith of the constanscbelness of God and the equality of Christ, and they discussed the question seven days, Constantine, sitting as chairman, on the throne. At the end of seven days, the discussion being ended, the question was put and one hundred and nineteen votes were thrown on each side, thus giving Constantine the deciding vote.

This was the establishing of Christianity, and with it a big quarrel ; and they have continued to quarrel ever since. They are like the sea ; they continue to cast up mud and dirt.

Well, Ariast was defeated and became an outcast, with all his followers, except those who recanted and embraced the true faith, as he called it.

Then Constantine saw the necessity of having a constitution and by-laws to guide his priests, as they had spread over many nations. So he selected the most prominent of them in every city to draft a constitution and by-laws.

They were to take the history of Josephus and

Philo and write out from the antiquity of the Jews a book to be called the Old Testament.

And from Josephus' wars of the Jews.

And Philo's history, called the "Contemplative Life," a book to be called the New Testament.

And all the priests who had no appointment were to have access to the written manuscripts to make whatever remarks they might think proper, to be called the Apocraphy to the Old and New Testament.

This is proved by the writers of the Apocraphy to the Old Testament referring to and explaining books that do not appear in the Bible.

My father said they were lost, but the fact is that they were not accepted by the council which met at Trent in 368 and decided by a vote what books should be called the Word of God. They would have done better had they rejected more than they did, especially the six books attributed to Moses and Joshua, written by Rabbi Helechiah; all but the first chapter of Genesis, which precedes the jumbling six books that make men live nearly a thousand years, so that they could date further back into antiquity.

There is no sane person to-day who does not know that human beings were not built in a manner that they could prolong life to that extent on this earth.

At the time Jacob went down into Egypt men lived at the longest only one hundred and thirty years, as I have stated in other parts of this book.

Judaism originated in Egypt as well as Christianity, so all the resurrections of the dead refer to the resurrection of the human body of flesh and blood until Paul's time, and nearly all the Israelites believed this earth was the heaven and the new Jerusalem was to be built here, and the Jews have talked about purchasing the Holy Land and building the new Jerusalem there.

I take the ancient history for just what it is worth to-day.

I will make a few remarks on Dr. Abbott's lecture on Christianity and Evolution. He is a profound Orthodox, a learned man, and is very liberal for one of that faith. I shall refer to his lecture on Evolution and Science. He is mostly right, and such talk will soon break the Orthodox boom.

But to his definition of Christianity I shall take some exceptions. I am a simple fisherman, but he must remember it was the ignorant fishermen of Galilee who put out the eyes of the philosophers and and learned men of their time, and as they have ruled Christianity since then if they have made no progress in science, so much the worse for Christianity.

Dr. Abbott says Christianity is civilized paganism. This is only half of the truth. Uncivilized Judaism is the other half, as I have told you.

And he speaks of "human ignorance in Jesus of Nazareth." How does he know that Jesus was ignorant? Who told him this?

He acknowledges that all the Bible is not true. He must be careful, or I shall get him where I have got many preachers stuck.

I have told you in this history of the origin of Christianity that Jesus was educated in Egypt, a pupil of Philo, with Judas of Galilee.

I must give you a little history older and truer than

his Bible. Josephus said of Jesus that he came from Egypt, was a smart man, far surpassing all other men. He called him the Egyptian false prophet and said that he went down to the seacoast of Tiberus and enlisted an army of several thousand of men of the lower grade, ignorant fishermen, common laborers, outlaws. (There was a multitude of them in and about Tiberus.)

He marched a part of his army up to the Mount of Olives, and there he proclaimed to them that he was sent of God, that he had a divine mission, which was to free the Jews from the Romans and become their King.

He enthused the army and led them on and attacked the Romans, but was defeated and ran away, embarked on a ship and escaped, but was subsequently caught, as I have described, and was executed, as it was proved that he had rebelled against the Romans, and claimed to be the Shilo, which so exasperated the Jews that they clamored for his blood and would have him crucified.

They were very religious after their kind.

I was talking with a very pious gentleman recently, and while speaking of Josephus he said it was a pity that he did not say more about Jesus than he did. He said it was great evidence for Christianity that he wrote what he did, referring to the eighteenth book of the "Antiquities of the Jews," third chapter, third verse, which is an entire interpolation. It breaks up the chain of connecting motives, and exposes the fraud, and then states that Josephus wrote that Jesus

135

was the Christ and did come back, and ate and drank with his disciples.

Only think that a Jew, and a priest at that, should acknowledge that impossibility, and write so much more after that and still be a Jew, and die in the faith.

I pity any man who is so blinded that he can't see such gross fraud because it seemed to favor his mistaken views.

I was taught during the first twenty years of my life by very learned preachers that my soul was not my own. So they preached, but I heard another more satisfactory idea. The preacher said I was not my own, but had been bought with a price. And he told what the price was that had been paid.

I found and believed that my Lord was in the slave trade, and I was his slave, and when I ended this life would have nothing to do but to sing. I was happy then, because I did not like to work so hard and fare so hard.

That was a very good doctrine. It made fair weather and a happy arrival in port at last.

I advise all my friends who think they must have some kind of religion to embrace it; not that it is any more true than any other, but, what is better, I have tried it and can vouch for it every time.

CHAPTER XVIII.

IT is now Christmas, and we find Jesus saying unto
the Pharisees: "Your father Abraham rejoiced
to see my day (December 25); he saw it, and was
glad. So I say unto my readers that John, the beloved disciple, rejoiced to see my day (December 26);
he saw it, and was glad. The jury had agreed.

John was a good boy, and Jesus loved him for his
good qualities. Think you that he would have trusted his mother in his hands for life if he had not been
good. John was conservative, and never committed
any overt act; but he was cruelly treated by Paul
and his followers becuse he would not go to all their
revival meetings.

John was then an old man and did not relish so
much excitement. But he had one friend who
possessed power, Barnabas, who declared that
the old man John Mark should go up to Jerusalem
with them to visit their friends.

But Paul declared that he should not. So they had
a sharp quarrel, and separated. Paul took Silas, and
they went their own way.

But Barnabas took Mark, whose Christian name
was John, and then John got so disgusted with Paul

137

and his clan, the Nicolatanes, that he left them and went to Ephesus and declaimed against them in the seven synagogues.

The churches were not Christian churches, as you have been told, as there were 666 of the Nicolatanes who had received the mark of that beast in their foreheads and in their right hands, and his name or the number of his name.

Now don't for one minute think that six hundred three score and six people could run seven Christian churches in seven different cities in Asia. John says that was the number, and he was there, and had been one of them, and ought to know, and he knew.

But when Paul heard what John was doing (he was then preaching to that great church at Corinth for the the first decade) he went to Ephesus and preferred a charge against John, and took him before the court, and summonsed the Nicolatanes of Ephesus and Pergemos, and proved John guilty of the charge, and had him sentenced to the isle of Patmos.

Now you are aware that ministers and good men who belonged to any clan were called angels. And any who differed from them were called beasts. Hence John called Paul a beast, and Paul called John a beast. Don't wonder. All learned men of any note know what I am writing is true.

Paul says in his first letter to the Corinthians, when he was begging a reinstatement as preacher, in the fifteenth chapter: "If, after the manner of men, I have fought with beasts at Ephesus, what advantage is it to me if the dead raise not?"

Our great light and explorer of the Holy Land

makes out Paul to be a pugilist or a gladiator, who went to Ephesus and fought with wild beasts. But where does he get his evidence? Surely not from the records.

Paul never was trained as a gladiator. So the explorer's theory blows to the wind, where the whangdoodles go and the screech owls make their nests. Their profound reverence to such men.

But let them be a little careful how they dabble with what they call sacred history without the proper opportunities to know truth from error.

I am not writing here a history of the book of Revelations, but positively say that it is not a book of the New Testament, and should not have been placed there, and was not considered as one for many years, until it was changed, having nine verses prefixed and several interpolations made.

And I only write this much to defend the good man John's character now he is dead. He received enough abuse from his ought-to-be friends, but many were not above taking his thunder which he hurled against them, and turning it against him, when he honestly intended it for them.

It is a great mistake for the credibility of the New Testament that the book of Revelations was added to it, as it is a Jewish record altogether, except the few alterations which are so glaring and self-evident that John never wrote them. They were fathered upon him by designing men, who wanted to have the book attached to the New Testament, as they had become ashamed of the Apocraphy which was then a part of the work. So the change was made.

You are aware that the book is composed of many books, by many writers.

But there are only four grand divisions, and they are the Old Testament and its Apocraphy, and the New Testament and its Apocraphy.

So you have but half of the original, now in use, but that is enough, and more than you can understand.

There is so much Bible printed to-day that the people cannot get along without quarrelling about it.

The more people know about it the more they quarrel about it. It has always been so, and probably it always will be so.

But most men to-day know but little about it, and it is well it is so; and they care still less, which is to their credit.

The earth still moves, and progression is still alive. God is ever present and distributes his glorious blessings broadcast with his hosts of angels in attendance. He has never forsaken his children, and he never will. No matter how many croakers there are around, he showers down his blessings all the same.

CHAPTER XIX.

THAT such a record should be copied by men blessed with sufficient sense to enable them to discern falsehood is surprising to me, and I think there are many whose reason is undeveloped in scripture.

If you should ask them some questions, like a few which I will name, they would be unable to answer you.

Here are some of the questions:

Which book of the Bible tells where God came from?

Who was the first man to commit murder?

What was the character of the house that God spared when Joshua took Jericho?

Or ask them about the characters of Abraham, Isaac, Jacob, Esau or Judah. They can't or won't tell you.

Ask them what they think of Solomon or David as moral men, and they are mum.

To all similar questions, mum is the word.

Ask them who kept a woman in Damascus in a house near the wall, and was three times whipped

141

and twice put in prison for his loose and lewd conduct and example.

And than ask them who killed Ananias and Sapphira, according to the witnesses given in the book.

Then asked who lied, cursed, swore and denied his best friend.

Shame on him! This was the worst thing I ever knew a fisherman to do.

But he had left his old trade, and was fishing for men, and he caught many.

Then ask what book tells who cast out devils by the power of devils, or deception.

And what book says that our Lord was crucified in Egypt. They all seem to know that he was crucified on Mount Calvary. None of us were there.

David, a man after God's own heart, tells us that God said in his anger that all men were liars.

And Paul says, "If through my lie the grace of God abounds, why should I be called a sinner, or why should I be called a liar?"

Paul was a droll dog, as men would say. Once I thought he was goody goody, hunky dory, and I could swallow him without greasing or using any gravy, speaking after the manner of men. But, then, I did not know him as I do now.

Since then I have been initiated into the rights and mysteries whereby we know each other.

I thank heaven or the gods for that fine nerve that gives me power to discern good from evil. I was born a know-nothing; that is, I did not know anything that I know now.

In my pilgrimage I have met men who seem to have no nerve or sense of feeling.

When I was a young man and had nothing to do on windy days (I was a fisherman, and windy days were leisure days) I went around and soldered pipes or fixed pumps, not as a hireling, but free work. It was not my trade.

On one occasion I was soldering for one of my neighbors. He was one of those men who have no nerve. The hot solder dropped on the floor. He quickly picked it up between his thumb and finger and put it on the pipe where it belonged.

I shouted to him when I saw what he was doing. He squeezed the melted solder flat to hold it while taking it from the floor. He said it did not burn him.

I think I felt more pain than he did.

I am describing the difference between men of feeling and those without it.

I once knew a man who was so negative that he really had no mind of his own, but did generally what he saw others do; yet he was a good sort of a man, capable, and smart when he had a leader.

Old men who are negative shake without wishing to do so. It is called paralysis, but it is really negativeness, no true nerve to steer the ship.

This man whom I describe lost the proper use or controlling power of his legs, that is, he could not control them, and they would run away with him sometimes when he was in the street and carry him where he did not want to go, and he sometimes had

to catch hold of a fence to stop himself. Marvel not
It is true.

He did not live to be very old. He died sometime
during the sixties.

Some year or more before he died I called to see
him one evening. He was sociable and glad to see
me, as one would say. I held a lighted lamp near
his eyes, and asked him if he observed any difference
or could see that there was a light near him. He said
he did not.

I felt sorry for and pitied him.

The foregoing is true to the letter.

I attach no blame to him. It was in accordance
with his organization. Yet had he known his weakness in that direction he might in some measure have
avoided so early a calamity.

I assure the friends of this man that I have the
best of feelings towards him and all his relatives,
always have had, and therefore do not give his
name.

I met a friend some years ago and asked him how he
was feeling, and he replied: " Bad. I gave up my
business nine years ago, and have done nothing but
shake since."

As this is a delicate matter to write on I will say
here and now that it is the mind that sees through
the optic nerve. By the abuse of the optic nerve men
become blind before their time. I realize this in my
own experience, as well as by observation.

Although I am writing now at the age of eighty I
have nearly lost the sight of my right eye, caused by
so much reading by lamp light during the past fall

and winter, devoting between three and four hours nearly every evening to reading. I am now determined not to read so much evenings hereafter.

Some of my religious friends say the Lord has eyes to give to the blind, but he does not give them to old men and women. So my advice to you is to take good care of your eyes and not depend upon the Lord giving you others, should you ever be so unfortunate as to need them.

He does not give two pair of eyes to one person, no more then he does two lives two one person, and that is impossible, no matter what we may think or dream concerning the theory.

I think I have given you the philosophy of life and death in a previous chapter. It is a fine point to talk about, two existences for one thing, or two lives for one person. Such foolish stuff has caused more wickedness and misery than all other causes put together.

Before we existed as individual beings we were a part of the earth, earthy. And now that we live and have an organized brain, we have become a part of the heavens, and are heavenly; with more omniscience or wisdom than any other living being, a complete microcosm, a living, positive proof that we were once dead matter, as it were, and shall be so again.

This proves my theory of the problem of one positive of the triune square, giving the other two, and cannot be successfully disputed; and that proves the one positive, as this proves one life and two deaths; and all who live have their part in the first resurrection. On such the second death cannot have any power, as I have stated in other parts of this book. I repeat it.

This is a very important part, and worth more to all my readers to know the truth and comprehend it than to know all about dreams, phantoms, imaginary spirits flying around.

Faith in things visionary has led men astray for thousands of years, and it is a wonder that people are as good as they are, after being kept in ignorance so long and taught what they cannot comprehend; and if it were not for our human laws no good people could live on this earth.

The misunderstanding of God's laws, is a serious matter. Every evil person has his own imaginary god, and would kill every other person who would not conform to his religion.

Don't marvel. Even our Puritans, as they were called, were so religious they did it.

Evil would reign triumphant if the god men had the power. Human law checks them.

CHAPTER XX.

I WILL add a few words to what I have said in other parts of this work, and give some ideas formulated by the great correspondent, Joseph Howard, Jr., as given in a letter written by him and printed in the Sunday Globe of January 10, 1892.

He enumerates a few of the many changes which may and probably will occur during the succeeding half century, and recapitulates some of the many discoveries made within the closing half century.

You can smile at some things I have told you of my own experience and cry "humbug," but that has been done since the making of history begun.

But I will tell you some things you know to be true. There are clairvoyants who pretend to go into a trance and see many things at a distance. That is a dreamy state or condition of the cerebellum, operating on an unconscious mind.

There are somnambulists, both men and women, who have got up out of their beds and walked in very dangerous places, and even returned home and

147

gone to bed without knowing that they had been out.

There are people who walk in their sleep at times, and you know it to be so. Therefore it is useless to resort to that old and familiar cry of " humbug" now.

The somnambulist does actually do and perform such acts by the aid of the cerebellum without the knowledge of the cerebrum.

This is just what I have told you repeatedly, that the instincts of the back brain could see without the aid of the optic nerve of intelligence, and where both are combined and controlled by the intelligence then both can be used for the benefit of mankind.

You will probably resort to the old shibboleth, and cry "humbug" again. Well, go on. All right.

We have a god given right to know as much as the animals and birds, and they know all I have claimed to know.

Men will come in the twentieth century and probably laugh at our ignorance as we laugh at the follies of those who have gone before us.

Now I give you Mr. Howard's prognostications:

" NEW YORK, Jan. 9—What a bully place to live in this world will be fifty years from now.

" And yet—

" Oh, there is always a yet and a but and an if· Isn't it odd. Of the half-million people who will read this letter to-morrow, very few can remember 50 years back, and doubtless scores of thousands will enjoy the millennial period of which I speak only 50 years from date. Fifty years ago there were no railways, no telegraph communications, no telephones, no street railways, no elevated roads, very few steam-

148

boats, no steamships of any consequence, no gas for illuminating purposes, no domestic utilization of the marvellous force, electricity.

"What of it?

"Well, this. If fifty years ago one had predicted that in 1892 we could cross the ocean in six days; could communicate with the farther ends of the globe by wire; could literally talk with friends in Chicago; we in Boston or New York could communicate with business people in London and receive an answer within the hour; could go from here to Boston in six hours, in cars brilliantly illuminated by electric fluid, turned on or off as water is made to flow or stop, he would have been regarded a lunatic.

"Now, it is impossible for us to conceive what improvements there are ahead of us, precisely as it was for them to forecast the marvellous advantages which you and I enjoy and think nothing of.

"Custom is everything.

"Our churches are opened to rich, and virtually closed against the poor. It is all nonsense to say that Christian charity welcomes every man, no matter what his garb, and that ordinary decency furnishes every woman a seat, no matter about her hat. Come with me to our great churches on our principal avenues and I will find you rudeness emphasized, discourtesy exaggerated. From the surpliced parson in his little box to the swollen, paunched sexton in the vestibule, there is a feeling, ' I am holier than thou.'

"Why?

"Because my clothes cost more.

"Don't deny it. It is, I know it; you see it, you

know it, and it is there, it seems to me, where an improvement ought to begin.

"It is in these public places, conspicuous by their flagrant disregard of the first principle of Christianity. 'Do unto others as you would have others do unto you,' that the improvement should be begun.

"However, in this 50 years from now, when my obituary will be a thing of the long past, and you young people will be the force and factors, there will be developed by art and science and inventive ingenuity improvements over the physical aids and abetments we enjoy as marked as these are an improvement and an advance over the crudities and discomforts of the past. One is almost tempted to believe that the fable story of the Persian carpet may come true, when, stepping upon a rug of small dimensions, a simple wish will transport the owner to any desired part of the earth.

"Every man will unquestionably have his electric-push wagon, his flying-machine, his favorite balloon, his mode of communicating with Tom, Dick and Harry, not to mention Sarah, Mary and Jane, and to men who study mental phenomena it won't seem particularly odd if, in that not so very remote period, men can read each other's thoughts.

"That, by the way, is not such a wonderful development after all.

"We understand our children, we read the little fellow's mind. Putting this and that together, we don't have to read his countenance to know what he wants, what he is thinking, up to a certain point, so, as compared with the advance made in telegraphy with the wonderful conveniences placed in the hands of our great organization by the Edisonic intellect, making a progress from the rude, crude mechanisms of 30 years, the studying, the reading and the clean cut apprehension of the minds of our fellows will not be such a wonderful indication of creative ability after all.

"I should hate to have some people know just what I think of them, because a catastrophe would result, but I am now talking of 50 years from now, when neither they nor I will have much to say about the affairs of the mundane sphere."

CHAPTER XXI

PROMETHEUS was a deity who united the divine and human nature in one person, and was confessedly "both God and man "—perfect God and perfect man, of a reasonable and human flesh subsisting; equal to the father as touching his godhead, but inferior to the father as touching his manhood; who, although he was God and man, yet was he not two, but one Prometheus; one, not by conversion of the godhead into flesh, but by taking the manhood into God; one altogether, not by confusion of substance, but by unity of person; for as the reasonable soul and flesh is one man, so God and man is one Prometheus; who, for us men and our salvation, came down from heaven, and was incarnate, and was made man, and was crucified also for us, under force and strength; he suffered, and descended into hell, rose again from the dead, he ascended into heaven, and sitteth on the right hand of the Father, God Almighty.

Thus far the Pagan and the Christian credenda ran hand in hand together; and it is a more than striking coincidence that the name Prometheus should be directly synonymous with the Logos, or Word of God, an epithet applied by St. John to the God and man or demi-deity of the Gospel, from before-hand, and care, or council; hence directly signifying the Christian deity, Providence, which we see emblemized as an eye surrounded with rays of glory, and casting its beams of light upon the affairs of our world. Indeed, under this designation, he continues to this day a more fashionable deity than the Logos of St. John. We find acknowlegdments of dependence on Divine Providence, and the blessing of Providence, or Prometheus, spoken of in our British parliament, occurring in his majesty's speeches, and received with the most respectful sentiment from one end of the kingdom to the other, where the introduction of the name of Jesus Christ, in the place of that of Prometheus or Providence, would be received with an universal smirk of undisguised contempt.

The best information of the character, attributes, and actions of this deity, is to be derived from the beautiful tragedy of Prometheus Bound, of Æschylus, which was acted in the theatre of Athens, 500 years before the Christian era, and is by many considered to be the most ancient dramatic poem now in existence. The plot was derived from materials even at that time of an infinitely remote antiquity. Nothing was ever so exquisitely calculated to work upon the feelings of the spectator. No author ever displayed greater powers of poetry, with equal strength of judgment, in supporting through the piece the august character of the divine sufferer. The spectators themselves were unconsciously made a party to the interest of the scene; its hero was their friend, their benefactor, their creator, and their saviour; his wrongs were incurred in their quarrel—his sorrows were endured for their salvation; "he was wounded for their transgressions, and bruised for their iniquities; the chastisement of their peace was upon him, and by his stripes they were healed." (Isaiah, liii., 5.) "He was oppressed and afflicted, yet he opened not his mouth." The majesty of his silence, whilst the ministers of an offended God were nailing him by the hands and feet to Mount Caucasus, could be only equalled by the modesty with which he relates, while hanging on the cross, his services to the human race, which had brought on him that horrible crucifixion:—

> "I will speak,
> Not as upbraiding them, but my own gifts
> Commending. 'Twas I who brought sweet hope
> T' inhabit in their hearts—I brought
> The fire of heaven to animate their clay :
> And through the clouds of barbarous ignorance
> Diffused the beams of knowledge. In a word,
> Prometheus taught each useful art to man."

In answer to a call made on him, to explain how his philanthropy could have incurred such a terrible punishment, he proceeds :—

> "See what, a god, I suffer from the gods!
> For mercy, to mankind, I am not deemed
> Worthy of mercy; but in this uncouth
> Appointment, am fixed here,
> A spectacle dishonorable to Jove!

On the throne of heaven scarce was he seated,
On the powers of heaven
He showered his various benefits, thereby
Confirming his sovereignty; but for unhappy mortals
Had no regard, but all the present race
Willed to extirpate, and to form anew.
None, save myself, opposed his will. I dared,
And boldly pleading, saved them from destruction—
Saved them from sinking to the realms of night;
For which offence, I bow beneath these pains,
Dreadful to suffer, piteous to behold!"

In the catastrophe of the plot, his especially professed friend, Oceanus, the Fisherman, as his name
Petræus indicates (Petræus was an interchangeable
synonyme of the name Oceanus), being unable to
prevail on him to make his peace with Jupiter, by
throwing the cause of human redemption out of his
hands, " forsook him and fled." None remained to be
witnesses of his dying agonies, but the chorus of ever
amiable and and ever-faithful women which also
bewailed and lamented him (Luke, xxiii., 27), but
were unable to subdue his inflexible philanthropy.
Overcome at length by the intensity of his pains,
he curses Jupiter in language hardly different in
terms, and but little inferior in sublimity to the " Eloi,
Eloi, lama sabacthani!" of the Gospel. And immediately the whole frame of nature became con-
vulsed; the earth shook, the rocks rent, the graves
were opened; and, in a storm that seemed to threaten
the dissolution of the universe, the curtain fell on the
sublimest scene ever presented to the contemplation

of the human eye—a dying God! The Christian muse has inspired our modern poets with no strains on this theme, but such as bear the character of plagiarism, parody, or paraphrase on the Greek tragedy. A worshipper of Prometheus would look in vain through all our collections of sacred poetry for a single idea which his own forms of piety had not suggested, or a single phrase whose reference would not seem to him, to have as direct an application to the god-man of Æschylus, as to the Jesus of the Evangelists :

> " Lo, streaming from the fatal tree,
>   His all-atoning blood!
> Is this the infinite? 'Twas he—
>   Prometheus, and a God!
> Well might the sun in darkness hide,
>   And veil his glories in,
> When God, the great Prometheus, died,
>   For man, the creature's sin."

The preternatural darkness which attended the crucifixion of Prometheus was natural enough as exhibited on the stage, and is beautifully described in the language of the tragedy. Nor is there any difficulty in conceiving, that when the mighty effect of so deep a tragedy on the feelings and sentiments of the audience became an inexhaustible source of wealth to the performers, there would be found those who would be shrewd enough to discover the policy of enhancing and perpetuating so profitable an impression on the vulgar mind, by maintaining that there was much more than a mere show in the business; that it was an exhibition of circumstances that had really happened; that Prometehus was a real personage and had actually done, and suffered, and spoken as in so lively a manner had been set before them; that the tragedy was a gospel put into metre; and that nothing but "an evil heart of unbelief" could induce any man to doubt "the certainty of those things wherein he had been instructed." It is probably no more than a figure of speech, though certainly very injudiciously chosen, in which Origen calls the crucifixion of Christ the most awful tragedy that was ever acted.

But the pretence of the reality of the event would break down, in the judgment of the better-informed, from the total want of evidence to support that part of the detail, which, had it been real, could not have wanted the clearest and most constraining demonstration. The darkness which closed the scene on the Prometheus, was easily exhibited on the stage, by putting out the lamps; but when the tragedy was to become history, and the fiction to be turned into fact, the lamp of day could not be easily disposed of. Nor can it be denied that the miraculous darkness which the Evangelists so solemnly declared to have attended the crucifixion of Christ, labors under precisely the same fatality of an absolute and total want of evidence.

Gibbon, in his usual strain of scarcasm and irony, keenly asks, "How shall we excuse the supine inattention of the pagan and philosophic world to those evidences which were presented by the hand of Omnipotence, not to their reason, but to their senses?

This miraculous event, which ought to have excited the wonder, the curiosity, and the devotion of mankind, passed without notice in an age of science and history. It happened during the lifetime of Seneca and the elder Pliny, who must have experienced the immediate effects, or received the earliest intelligence of the prodigy. Each of these philosophers, in a laborious work, has recorded all the great phenomena of nature—earthquakes, meteors, comets and eclipses, which his indefatigable curiosity could collect; both the one and the other have omitted to mention the greatest phenomenon to which the mortal eye has been witness since the creation of the globe."— Gibbon, vol. 2, ch. 15, p. 379.

This objection of Gibbon is answered by Bishop Watson, in a double-entendre paragraph, which opens with the curious word to the wise, that " though he was aware he was liable to be misunderstood in what he was going to say, yet Mr. Gibbon would not misunderstand him." Then follows the most extraordinary declaration of his own (a bishop's) faith, " that however mysterious the darkness at the crucifixion might have been, he had no doubt the power of God was as much concerned in its production as it was in the opening of the graves, and the resurrection of the dead bodies of the saints that slept, which accompanied that darkness."—[Third letter to Gibbon, last paragraph.] Another way of saying, that every sensible man must perceive that one part of the story was just as probable as the other, or that it was a romance altogether. The good Bishop ventured to trust his security to the well-proved truth of the

adage, " None are so blind as those who will not see."
The immoral and mischievous tendency of the doctrine of atonement for sin, so acceptable to guilty minds,
and so eagerly embraced by the greatest monsters of
iniquity, had been preached by self-interested priests,
and reprobated by all who wished well to mankind,
long before the doctrine was deduced from the
Christian Scriptures, long before those Scriptures
are pretended to have been written.

Betore the period assigned to the birth of Christ,
the poet Ovid had assailed the demoralizing delusion
with the most powerful shafts of philosophic scorn :

" Cum sis ipse nocens, moritur cur victima pro te?
Stultitia est morte alterius sperare salutem."

"When thou thyself art guilty, why should a victim
die for thee? What folly it is to expect salvation
from the death of another."

No particle of difficulty remains, then, in accounting
for the fact, that in that portion of the Acts of the
Apostles in which the miraculous style is discontinued,
and we so clearly trace the probable and most likely
real adventures or journal of a missionary sent out
from the college of the Egyptian Therapeuts joined
on as an appendix to some fragment of their sacred
legends which detailed the mystical adventures of the
supposed first founders of their order, whose example
the missionary was to have continually before him,—
we should read, that when the apostolic Therapeut
attempted to preach his doctrine of "Jesus Christ and

him crucified," at Athens, he found that the Athenians were already in possession of all he had to communicate, and that what he was endeavoring to set off as a doctrine newly revealed was with them a very old story. He brought to their ears "no new things." The Epicurean and Stoical philosophers were more at home than himself upon that subject, and called him "a babbler," the very term that most expressively designates the character of a doting ignoramus, who, in the arrogance of his own conceit, will be for ever foisting up old stories of a hundred thousand years' standing, and swearing that they had occurred in his own experience, and had happened to nobody else but some particular acquaintances of his.

The majority, however, carried the vote that he should have a fair hearing, and Paul was allowed to preach in the Areopagus. The previous rebuke he had received had completely subdued his impertinence; he no more presumed to lay claim to originality in the crucifying story. He preached pure Deism, quoted their own poets, and ventured not once so much as to mention his Jesus, or to make an illusion that could be construed as referring to him rather than to any other of the god-men or man-gods who had risen from the dead as well as he. (Acts, xvii.)

Prometheus, exactly answering to the Christian personification Providence, is, like that personification, used sometimes as an epithet synonymous with the Supreme Deity himself. The Pagan phrase, " Thank Prometheus," like the Christian one, " Thank Providence," its literal interpretation, meant exactly the same as "Thank God." Thus in the Orphic Hymn to Chronus or Saturn, we have this sublime address to the Supreme Deity under his name Prometheus, "Illustrious, cherishing Father, both of the immortal gods and of men, various of counsel, spotless, powerful, mighty Titan, who consumest all things, and again thyself repairest them, who holdest the ineffable bands throughout the boundless world; thou universal parent of successive being, various in design, fructifier of the earth and of the starry heaven, dread Prometheus, who dwellest in all parts of the world, author of generation, tortuous in counsel, most excellent, hear our suppliant voice, and send of our life a happy blameless end." Amen!

A free poetical version of a hymn to Diana, expressive of her attributes, as generally believed and worshipped about the time of St. Paul, to the measure of the Sicilan Mariner's Hymn:—

"Great is Diana of the Ephesians."—Acts, xix., 34.

———

"Great Diana! huntress queen!
Goddess bright, august, serene!
In thy countenance divine
Heaven's eternal glories shine.

Thou art holy! thou alone,
Next to Juno, fill'st the throne!
Thou for us on earth wast seen—
Thou, of earth and heav'n the queen!

They to thee who worship pay,
From thy precepts never stray;
Chaste they are, and just and pure,
And from fatal sins secure;

Peace of mind 'tis theirs to know,
To thy blessed sway who bow;
Chastest body, purest mind—
Will, to will of God resign'd;
Conquest over griefs and cares;
Peace—for ever peace, is theirs.

O bright goddess! once again
Fix on earth thy heav'nly reign;
Be thy sacred name ador'd,
Alters rais'd, and rites restor'd!

But if long contempt of thee
Move thy sacred deity
This so fond request to slight
Beam on me, on me, thy light.

Thy adoring vot'ry, I
In thy faith will live and die;
And when Jove's supreme command
Call me to the Stygian strand,

I no fear of death shall know,
But with thee contented go;
Thou my goddess, thou my guide,
Bear me through the fatal tide;

Land me on th' Elysian shore,
Where nor sin, nor grief is more—
Life's eternal blest abode,
Where is virtue, where is God."

First published in the Author's Clerical Review, in
Ireland.

THE PRAYER OF SIMPLICIUS.

There is a most beautiful prayer of the Pagan
Simplicius, generally given at the end of Epictetus'
Enchiridion, and almost the model of that used in
our Communion Service, "O Almighty God, to whom
all hearts are open, all desires known," etc. The
ideas are precisely the same; the words and the
machinery alone are a little varied. I find a ready-
made poetical version of this in Johnson's Rambler:

" O thou, whose pow'r o'er moving worlds presides,
Whose voice created, and whose wisdom guides!
On darkling man in pure effulgence shine,
And cheer the clouded mind with light divine.
'Tis thine alone, to calm the pious breast
With silent confidence and holy rest.
From thee, great Jove! we spring, to thee we tend,
Path, Motive, Guide, Original, and End!"

CHAPTER XXII.

IN 1833 I introduced trolling for halibut and fished in that way one winter, in the gully north of Race Point, and kept it a secret, fisherman like, and caught about three shares of fish to my neighbor's one.

The next winter all the neighbors knew it, and adopted that method of catching halibut, and in the following spring I introduced that form of fishing on Nantucket shoals and along the back of Cape Cod and followed it for several winters.

In 1838 I introduced the netting of mackerel with gill nets, at Sandy Point, Pleasant Bay, Chatham and Nantucket.

In 1841 my brother and myself fitted out the schooner Lucy Mary for a mackerel voyage to the Azore islands. It proved to be a failure, as my brother did not arrive at the islands in season to make a catch. They were not mackerel.

In 1844 I introduced netting mackerel at Monhegan and subsequently at other points on the coast of

Maine, and also turned my attention to fresh fishing and trolling halibut on Nantucket shoals, and could catch as many halibut as four or five New London smacks could in the old way. So I continued in that business for several years, netting mackerel in the summer season.

In 1848 I brought the first mackerel ever received on ice in Boston. It was in the month of August. I took them in the sloop smack American Eagle.

In the same year I introduced the jib topsail, which made the smack go very fast in light winds. It was the first jib topsail ever seen on a fishing vessel or yacht in Massachusetts.

In 1852 I had built a schooner smack of eight tons, called the Golden Eagle. She was constructed to carry two cargoes at one time, and she was a success. I could and did carry the largest load of live lobsters that any smack ever carried into New York, and as large a freight of iced halibut and cod on the well deck as any smack carried to New York.

When I fished on Nantucket shoals I took in from 2500 to 3000 lobsters and went on to the shoals and fished from three to five days, and then proceeded to New York. If I went to Georges Bank, then on my way to New York, I called at Provincetown and took in my lobsters, bought of the fishermen, as they always had plenty at that time.

In the winter I run the schooner as a packet from Provincetown to Boston.

In 1853 I bought a small schooner called the Wave Crest, and made a very successful year's work in netting mackerel at Monomoy and Monhegan.

Then I gave up fishing and bought into the Central Wharf Company, with Mr. E. S. Smith, Mr. W. A. Atkins and Mr. Amasa Smith, and took the inspection department.

I worked two years, and the third year, my health failing me, I employed Mr. W. A. Atkins to take my place, as he had previously sold out his interest to Captain Atkins Nickerson, and had been to Springfield a year or so. At the close of the year I sold my interest to him, and purchased a small schooner and went to sea for my health, as it was not healthy to go without bread. I recovered my health in this way.

The schooner was called the Mary E. She was a shell of a thing.

I was successful for two years in running fresh mackerel to Boston in ice. There were others in the same business then—that was in 1859-61.

In the summer of 1861 I bought a schooner which was then being built at Kennebunkport, and called her Rebecca N. Atwood, for my daughter.

The first thirteen days I sailed her I cleared for myself $550. She was a racer for those days. No market boat could beat her. She yielded me some two hundred dollars on the first two trips, on her speed over others, I made in her to Monhegan, as I beat all the boats on the route and saved the Friday morning market both times, and no other boat arrived in season to save the morning market.

The boats which I contended with which had fresh mackerel in ice were the Minnehaha, Yankee Maid, Daniel C. Baker and E Pluribus Unum of Swampscott.

The next winter, 1862, I built the Cosmos; in the spring I built the Golden Rule, and run her as an express packet, carrying passengers from Provincetown to Boston.

I modelled another schooner, and she was built by David Clark of Kennebunkport. He built the schooner Susan West from my first model, in 1863.

I left Kennebunkport July 13, 1863, with the said schooner. My crew was Captain J. T. Sparks and his wife as passengers, and my wife and daughter. They comprised all who were on board. The wind was light northeast. It was in the morning, and Captain Sparks remarked that he never saw a vessel go so fast with such a light breeze before.

In the afternoon we saw the Cape, and the wind had hauled out east, southeast, and as we drew near the race we saw a large schooner yacht coming up the back side. So we put the schooner in the wind and swayed up fore and aft. We had all our bunting flying, as we were bound home, and it was the first day that the schooner had sailed. As we held up around the race the yacht hauled up in our wake, and hooked on for a race. It was head tide and the wind was dead ahead, and five and one-half miles to beat, and three and one-half miles of the wind. We readily preceived that we outwinded her, and dropped her, and she tacked every time we did, but kept falling to the leeward, so that when we weathered Wood End she was quite a distance to leeward, and did not pass Wood End until we were nearly across the harbor.

When we shot alongside of my wharf, Captain

Sparks said: "There is the yacht just coming in the range of the fort on Long Point, two miles away." It proved to be the yacht America.

It was a fair sail, and I beat her more than a mile and a half. But she was in the government employ, and sailors were managing her. That somewhat accounts for it. There is a great difference in those who think they know how to sail a yacht or fishing craft. There is a science in boat sailing as well as in modelling.

I was quite well pleased when the Puritan sailed the race with the Genesta, as Captain Aubrey Crocker, formerly of Provincetown, was sailing master. The wind was light at first, and I saw that he had the science of sailing a craft, as he outpointed all the other boats. That gave him more wind.

I saw by the account of all his movements that he had the science that I had, but I don't say he took it from me, although he was a near neighbor to me when he lived in Provincetown, and sailed with me when I was in the Cosmos. I think then he was 16 or 17 years old. He was very quiet, and asked no questions, but was a close observer.

I sometimes explained somethings to the crew, but the older men did not take any stock in what I told them, fishermen like. They thought they knew it all.

At the same time they knew I could sail a boat or vessel faster than they could, and the most of them were willing to acknowledge it, as in all the races which I sailed I came out first best, until I sailed my keel boat with some centerboard boats belonging in

Connecticut, and they beat me every time This was at Monomoy.

I bought a centerboard boat and brought her home and named her the " Reaper." She would discount any boat we had. She was the first centerboard boat that ever came to Provincetown. Since then there have been a great many built for all purposes.

There was a lad went out with me in the schooner Mary E., to take lessons, when I was on a short trip, fresh fishing. He was somewhat out of health, and did not grow to manhood. He had a keen nerve for yachts, modelling and sailing miniature yachts the best of any one in town, and could beat all others at it.

In sailing a yacht from a light breeze until the wind is blowing seven knots, four points is the criterion, but I have occasionally sailed three and one-half points from the wind with success, but it is not often that it can be done unless the wind is light and the water very smooth.

None but the most skilful can be a successful boat sailer. It requires quickness of thought and accuracy of judgment.

Here is the rule for sailing with a wind blowing under seven miles an hour: Trim your sails as they should be. This requires art and skill, as well as experience.

Start with your course about five points from the wind, and as the craft gets her best speed then let her come slowly nearer towards the four points. By so doing you increase the wind, and so hold your speed, or gain it until you come to four points, and if the speed does not lessen you can come a bit nearer, closely observing the speed of your craft. If you find it has deadened then give her a hard full and gain it as quick as you can, and lose no time.

This is the science of windward work in yacht sailing.

I never sailed a yacht, but I have beat a great many, of all classes except cutters, there not being any at that time.

In 1869 I invented the launching topmasts, and received a patent for seventeen years.

It was a success, but I was not able to introduce it. I had no skill in that direction.

I built a fishing schooner, 105 tons, and applied the rig. She would sail faster than any other vessel of her model from a calm to a gale of wind, and faster even than much sharper vessels.

The topmast came down and connected with the fife rail, and served as double masts, the other mast, being shorter than usual, and carried less heavy canvas and did not require reefing so often.

All yachts and many clipper fishing craft which are built now have launching topmasts, but they don't connect with the rail or standard. It would be much better if they did, and they will come to it, sooner or later, in the twentieth century.

I think it was about 1870 or 1871 that William Weld, who had a large schooner yacht, received a challenge for a race. He was going to have her masts taken out and longer ones put in. I saw the schooner at East Boston. Her masts and lower sails were just right for my rig for racing. I went to him and offered him my patent free if he would rig his schooner with my rig. It would save considerable expense, and would not cost him half as much; but he declined.

Then I told him I would guarantee to pay all his expenses, if he was beaten, if he would let me sail the yacht, and I would not charge anything for my services in any event. In this I had no success.

So I rigged a small market boat and went to Gloucester to try to introduce the rig, knowing that it would be of great advantage to Gloucester, as they were just beginning the Grand Bank halibuting. The craft would sail faster then she could with the old rig, but I could not get any one to adopt it.

If they had adopted it they would have saved a great many lives and many vessels from being wrecked and lost, and would also have made much more money, and their vessels would have made quicker passages and have been much safer.

But the time will come when men will know more than they do now, and they will laugh at our foolish ways as we laugh at those who lived before our day. The world is progressing, and the earth has moved ever since the days of Joshua, and will continue to . move in the ages to come.

It is a fact that it moved just the same in Joshua's time, only the people did not know it.

As the fish curers in Provincetown pickle nearly all their Bank fish (and have been doing so for many years), I will tell you who pickled the first Grand Bank fish in Provincetown, where that business begun.   They pickled Georges fish in Gloucester, but not Bank fish.

I think it was about 1854 that J. W. Smith was master of the schooner D. C. Smith.   He sailed in the schooner for me two fares to the Grand Banks. The price for fish was very low.   He went on two fares, and on the last one secured only 300 quintals.

When I had them half cured, there being no sale for fish at that time, I told him that I would buy the fish as they were, without any more drying and give him the price received for the last sales, so we could settle up the voyage, as it was a hard one, and he and his crew could have what little was coming to them.   He accepted my proposition, and the next day weighed off the fish to me, and I put them in pickle.

That was some time in October.   I kept them in until the middle of February.   Then I took them out and subsequently put them on the flakes one short day, and piled them away.

On the twenty-second of February a New York agent came over to Long Point and bought them at a good price, so that I made a fair profit.   They overrun some ten quintals more than when I bought them, and that added made a good speculation for a small trade.

That was the beginning of pickling Bank fish in Provincetown.

I pickled quite a number of fares while I carried on the Banking business in that town, but the Banking business is like the tide there.   Sometimes it is flood tide, and if high of course it is prosperous and comes high; but ebb tide is sure to follow and go very low sometimes.

That was my experience for more than sixty-two years during which I was a resident there, when I was run out and the bottom dropped out of business.

I left Provincetown without a dollar to my name to enter the commission business in Boston. It was an uphill road to travel at my age, but nothing daunted I commenced my work in earnest.

I had opposition to contend with, and much business on my hands for the benefit of the fisheries, in behalf of my shippers, without any remuneration for services rendered, before many committees of the Legislature, Board of Railroad Commissioners, Board of Health and other city officials.

I have the satisfaction of knowing that I was never defeated there on any remonstrance or the repeal of any law passed against the rights of fishermen that I carried before the Legislature.

Some Boston gentlemen made me generous presents in the shape of dollars for the good service I had rendered them, for which I give them thanks. It has enabled me to procure a nice comfortable home in Malden, and I have a modest income, sufficient for my daily wants, and now I have nothing to trouble or worry me in this world, nor in any other.

I have fought a good, practical fight, and have laid up treasures enough to feed and clothe me the remainder of my days, and have the satisfaction of knowing that I have done right, according to the best of my knowledge and ability. With the same knowledge I might have made and kept more money,

173

but that would not have given me the satisfaction and peace of mind and clear conscience.

This book has not been written for money, but at the earnest solicitation of many friends who desired it as a keepsake.

If money had been my object of course I should have done as many other book writers have done, skipped over the truth when it was too strong for many readers. They want a theory that will agree with their feelings and assure them that they shall have what they will never get; but there is one thing in their favor, and that is that they will never know it. That is no disappointment.

CHAPTER XXIII.

I WILL now relate a few incidents of my past life, selecting only a very few of the many, and only those to which living witnesses can testify to their truthfulness.

I will go back to the period embraced in the years from 1843 to 1846, during which time I was running a small sloop smack, catching fish and taking them alive to the Boston market, principally cod.

During the several winters when we had made trips, and the wind breezed up from the southeast, with snow, if there was time sufficient to carry the craft to Boston before it was dark, I always squared away for Boston. But all the other smacks harbored at Provincetown. The next morning found us in Boston, with a cold northwest wind, a good time to sell our cargo.

We sold and delivered the fish and sailed for home before night, and the next morning found us at our moorings, close beside our neighbors ; they with their fish in, and we ready to go for another fare.

So you see the advantage we had. I had three excellent men with me, although they would not take such chances, but put all confidence in me, and never

175

hung back. It was a pleasure to have such men for a crew. They we all good pilots, but they have all gone the way of flesh. Peace be to their ashes. Their names were N. E. Atwood, my older brother; John Ginn and Philip Smith.

There are men in Provincetown who know the statements I make are true.

But I will mention one instance in this connection which has no living witness to corroborate it.

I think it was in the winter of 1845. We left Boston in the evening with a light southeast breeze. We always stood single watch in good weather. I took the first, and when we were at Long Island head I called Philip Smith, and as the weather looked a little threatening I did not take of my boats, nor clothes, but lay down in my berth and fell asleep.

Subsequently I heard Philip say " All hands on deck! A squall!" I sprung up the gang way, and Philip jumped and let go the mainsail halyards. The little craft's lee rail was well under. When we had got the sails both down, and all hands were on deck, I asked Philip where we were, and he replied:

"About half way from Boston Light to Point Allerton buoy."

"All right," said I, and I clapped the little craft before the wind, hustled the peak of the mainsail to the wind, and steered the craft through the winding channel into the Narrows, and anchored near Lovell's island, without having seen land, light or buoy, for it was very dark and thick snow, with a blizzard to help it.

I relate this incident because it illustrates the

connection of the instinctive with the cerebellum as applied to the cerebrum, giving accurate course and distance.

Be not surprised as you will find this phenomenon fully verified in what I am about to relate, and concerning which I shall give you evidence to substantiate all I say.

Whenever I have had occasion to blend the visionary with the real I have never made a mistake, nor ran a vessel ashore, nor missed my mark.

I will relate a circumstance bearing on this point. The steamer George Shattuck was new, I think, in the winter 1864. I was in Boston on business, and had occasion to take passage in the said steamer home. It was not a very propitious looking time. We left the city at the usual time, and when we got down to Minot's light house it began to snow and breeze fast. So I took the bearings and went into the cabin, as there were some thirty passengers, there being several ladies among them. Mrs. Smith, the captain's wife, was one of them.

She was very nervous, and said to me :

" Captain Atwood, we are going to have a dreadful time. The snow is so thick how can we find the way ? "

I said to her : "We are going to Provincetown. It is all right. No matter about the snow. It is uncomfortable, but we are sure of our port, and there is no danger."

This seemed to calm the agitation somewhat. I took my paper, but occasionally looked out, and kept the speed of the boat in my mind until I considered we were well over across the bay, when I took my overcoat to put on, as my brother, N. E., came into the cabin and said:

"Captain Smith wants to see you at the wheel house."

"Very well," said said I; I was just going up."

Now Captain Smith was a sea captain, but not much of a coast or packet pilot, but his two chief officers were good pilots. Mr. Samuel Kilburn, the mate, was a good bay pilot, and had run a vessel many years. The clerk, Mr. N. P. Holmes, now living, was a very good pilot. He had run as master of a packet from Provincetown many years. To him I refer you for the truth of this statement.

But Captain Smith was one of those men who did not care to call upon any of his officers for advice, but being intimately acquainted with me he preferred to call upon me, and did so.

When I arrived at the wheel house I said:

"Captain, how have you run since you left Minot's?"

He replied:

"Southeast by east."

I said:

"Swing her off four points south by east. We shall make Race Point inside of thirty minutes."

In about twenty-five minutes I said:

"Swing her off. There is the bell frame on Race Point, near the light house."

In a few minutes we were in smooth water. Then I said:

" Captain, I thank you for giving me an invitation to take part in this, for it gives me pleasure to render any assistance where it is needed."

I said this because I saw the captain's great anxiety, and I had relieved him of it.

I do not think he asked either of his officers for any advice as to how to steer the boat for Provincetown, as I never made any inquiry of them.

But Mr. N. P. Holmes can tell you whether he did or not. I think it was a great burden on him, and he ought to have consulted them, knowing they were good pilots. He needed advice, and without it he would have run the boat outside of the cape in a heavy easterly gale, and night approaching.

I think he felt it afterwards, as he mentioned the circumstance to me some eight or ten times during the remainder of his life.

At another time when I was a passenger he run into a thick fog, and made the Graves just in time to stop the boat and avoid striking the rocks.

When we knew we had passed Minot's, and were close to Hardings, Mr. Holmes, the clerk, said to me:

" We are in the channel and ought to haul up, west northwest."

I said:

" Yes, and if he runs northwest much longer he will be on the Graves."

He never was such a pilot as Provincetown now has in Captain John Smith of the steamer Longfellow.

It is a blessing to passengers to know that the captain is a pilot. I never give myself any uneasiness in thick weather when I am on board the Longfellow, and never trouble myself to look out.

Well, I will mention another occasion when I regretted to be forced to take the position which I did. It was when Captain R. Stevens ran the packet schooner Cosmos, and Mr. Samuel Kilburn was mate, and John W. Atwood was clerk.

I think it was in 1862 or 1863. I had occasion to go to Boston. It was the first part of January, and a Saturday. It was very cold, and the vapor was so thick we could not see half way from Commercial wharf to East Boston.

Captain Stevens said to Mr. Kilburn:

"Get in what freight you have and haul around the corner before the vessel grounds."

When he had gone, I said to Mr. Kilburn:

" I hope you will ground."

He replied:

" I hope so, too; but I must obey orders."

I said to him:

" There will be no fit time for any vessel to cross the bay to-night, and you are having the schooner loaded under water."

We left Commercial wharf at a quarter past three in the afternoon, and at that time it was blowing a gale out in the bay.

They put a close reef in the mainsail, and when we had arrived at Point Allerton buoy I went down and rigged up warm and put on an oil suit belonging to the Captain, as he had all he could do to look after the passengers, and did not come on deck during the whole night.

Well, I took the wheel at the bell buoy at Hardings ledge. I said when I took it :

" I shall not leave the wheel until we arrive in Provincetown, if the little schooner keeps above water long enough to get there."

A packet, you know, is never overloaded, like our horse cars.

I recently rode on a horse car where there were fifteen men and one boy on the rear platform at one time. It was very difficult for me to retain my position, and avoid being pushed over the back rail, owing to the crush, although holding on with both hands.

Well, I will describe the schooner that we had to cross the bay in. She was stowed full of freight over her winter ballast. She had sixty barrels of beef and pork, and four hogsheads of molasses on deck, which was only a few inches above the water. The vessel drew about eleven feet. All the water that came on deck to stay turned to ice.

We had thirty-five passengers on board, and some ten or twelve of them were seamen, and you can be sure they were on deck to stay. No seaman who thought any thing of his life would leave the deck until we were out of danger. They were all ready to execute any order that might be given them.

When we were nearly across I placed two men who I knew were trustworthy and sure at the main halyards, and told them to have both through and peak halyards so they could be let go at a second's warning, and the others were to haul in the main sheet until the boom was jibed, and then jump to the halyards and put the mainsail up quick.

As the main boom was on the starboard side it had to be jibed if we made the breakers on the back side bars. I intended for the vessel to be headed off shore without going once her length after breakers were discovered if she did not strike bottom.

I sent word forward just what to do, and orders to do it quick, if breakers were seen. I said:

"Men, we are now ready, and shall probably make Race Point in ten minutes."

John Winslow, a passenger, went up on the third hoop on the mainsail, and had not been there more than seven or eight minutes when he sung out:

"Light O right ahead!"

I swung her off a point, and the next revolution he and others shouted:

"Light O one point off the weather bow!"

It was seen fore and aft. The third flare-up it was right abeam and close to.

So we proceeded, and I was very glad to be relieved of the anxiety.

We then hoisted a small jib, and when we came around Long Point, to beat up the harbor, it was very dark, when something within seemed to say:

"Time to tack."

I ordered "Ready about," and put the wheel astarboard, when she quickly shot past a schooner that was at anchor. I said:

"Mr. Kilburn, didn't you see that vessel?"

"No, sir," was the reply.

In three seconds more we should have struck the schooner, and probably have sunk her.

There was no one on board of her, and she had no light up.

Well, we arrived at central wharf at twelve o'clock and landed the passengers.

I do not remember many of them who are now living. I think Moses Turner was one. But all who were on board will remember the circumstances when they read this account.

The next morning was Sunday, and when the citizens came down to the wharf and saw the vessel, they said:

"Here is the Cosmos. Well, that was Atwood. That vessel never would have crossed the bay in such a night if he had not been on board." (That was probably so.)

But I took it rather as disparagement then praise, as I did not think I was such a fool as to take such chances when there was no need of it. And I have felt angry with myself every time I have thought of it since—that I had not protested against the vessel leaving. If I had not owned the vessel, and have had a son on board, I should have walked up and stopped in Boston.

So many similar circumstances have caused me to be an old man at eighty, because I have so often drawn the intuitive powers of the cerebellum, which did not belong to me to use only in very extreme cases between life and death.

But having the key that unlocks the mystery box that contains the interior vision and blend it with the intelligence of the cerebrum and use it in connection to give whatever is needed, be it course and distance, from one object to another; or if any thing be lost, by the same aid it can be found, as I have proven many times. It is a wonder, and it has surprised me many times; but it belongs to man, and neither spirit nor angel has anything to do with it.

I will give you the particulars of another occurrence. I think it was during the next winter. Captain Stevens commanded the Cosmos, Captain John Burt was mate, and J. W. Atwood was clerk. Alfred Nickerson was one of the crew, I think.

We left Provincetown at 9 o'clock in the morning.

I was a passenger, with some ten or twelve others, principally seamen.

As we sped away from Steamboat wharf the pilot boat Marshal Tukey, No. 4, I think it was, started close behind us. The wind was southeast and light, and I urged the schooner along as fast as I could by trimming and the laying on of hands on the wheel, so when we were half way across toward the Minot we were a mile and a half ahead of the pilot boat, and it shut down with thick snow and began to breeze very fast.

I shaped our course for Scituate Point, made the lighthouse close aboard, then for South Entering rock, and timed the distance, Captain Elijah Doane standing in the gangway keeping time.

When the time was up we sighted the rock, hauled off northeast, saw the breakers on the Castor and Palock; then I steered her for Minot's, giving her seven minutes; when the time was up the lighthouse

184

was close aboard. Then I shaped her course for the Bell Boat, giving the time as twenty-seven minutes, but we had to shorten sail and I discovered it in twenty-nine minutes.

Then seven minutes to Point Auling buoy, which I saw just in time; and as the main boom was on the port side we had to haul down the mainsail and jibe. When we had jibed we saw Boston lighthouse close aboard.

Then I shaped her course for False Spit buoy, and Captain Stevens came aft and asked me how I was running.

I said: "West by south."

"Are you not running up too much?" he asked.

I said, "No"

In time we made the buoy, and every other one I run her for, clear to the city, and got in the dock, when it was quite dark; and when we were going by the end of the T we were running at the rate of six knots under bare poles.

But the pilot boat had to lay out all night.

Mr. Burt said:

"I am glad you came, as we should not have been here now if you had not come."

I said "No."

Than Captain Dan Conway and others said:

"You are the strangest man we ever saw. Can you see so much better than anybody else?"

I said: "No."

"Why, you saw everything first, and while some eight or ten men were nearer the object than you were."

Then I said I steered the vessel, stated the object I was running for and the time it would take to get there, and asked them if I had made a mistake.

They said I had not. I then told them that if I had made a mistake I should not have been the first person to see the object.

My readers will say that it was all chance, but how did it happen that I never missed my mark nor run a vessel ashore in those dark and thick times, and I have run a great many of them.

Some of my readers will believe many other things that they cannot understand, and can't put into practice.

Well, let every one be fully persuaded in his own mind, but he need not follow Paul, but have some manhood in himself.

I will give one more novel instance in my long career.

Some years ago I was running a little smack to Boston with lobsters. One afternoon I came out of Provincetown late, with light southeast winds. I had two passengers on board, N. E. Atwood and Captain T. L. Mayo of the firm of T. L. Mayo & Co. of Commercial street, Boston, now living.

As the fog became very thick at sunset, I shaped my course for the iron frame on Minot's ledge, the light having been previously wrecked and broken down, and the keepers drowned.

My two passengers went below, as I said we should be at the ledge about 9 o'clock. I had a small boy with me. It was smooth, and the smack was running five or six miles an hour. We both sat down on the deck. I listened, supposing I should hear the surf on the rocks. At five minutes before nine I told the boy to go and let down the square sail, as we called it (now called a spinnaker), and as he arose he said :

" Here is a buoy right alongside."

I put the helm hard aport, and as the two men came out of the gangway, the sails took back before the sail could be lowered, or the main guy be let go, and the sloop stopped. My brother let the guy go, and Captain Mayo hauled in the boom by taking all parts of the main sheet, and the boy had got the spinnaker down, and the frame work was not half the width of the smack away, and, as the current was setting over the rock against the iron strands, the hull struck. The heel struck the rock as we pushed her off with our hands and two eight foot oars. She started ahead and struck bottom three times. As we cleared the ledge the main toplift would have caught the crossbars ; I cut the fall and Captain Mayo jerked it clear, hauling the boom to windward. Then we squared away and went to Boston all right.

CHAPTER XXIV.

THERE is a fish which is called a dog. It is not a true fish. It has fins, but no scales. It is called cartilagenous. When it is pupped the mother nurses the little pup from a bottle until the little fish can feed itself.

There is another kind of a fish called a cat. It is a true fish, but it don't have kittens. It lays eggs and then goes off and leaves them to hatch themselves, the same as the Murs and Turs do that lay their eggs on the Macatine islands on the coast of Labrador.

We have another kind of fish called a crustacean, that lays her eggs and covers or sets on them as the domestic fowl which takes some three weeks for the chickens to come out, and when they are hatched they are as perfect in form as their mother is.

I had a hatching place where I hatched out many thousands. Even in one night I have hatched out more than one thousand, and strewed them along the coast from Cape Cod to Long Island Sound.

188

And there is another peculiar fish. It is called a monk fish. That was a name given to it long ago, probably on account of its great capacity for swallow· ing objects larger than its own body, as the monks of Egypt had the capacity of swallowing the whole creation, and then throwing it up again, as Jonah was hove up.

This may have been the fish that God created, or rather prepared, to swallow him, as I have taken from the stomach of one of them another fish of the same kind, and those boys who were with me all pronounced the one which was within the other as the largest and would weigh the most.

Fishermen call them "goose" fish. Perhaps the name was given them because one of them had swallowed a live goose; but whether so or not I am not able to say.

But I do know that one of them swallowed a large gull whole, feathers and all, as I took the gull from the fish's stomach. It was what we call a Colonel gull, and weighed about four pounds.

The gull was evidently swimming on the water when the fish swam along under him, and opened that great mouth of his, and Mr. Gull was taken in and done for.

But it was too much for the fish, as he lost his balance, turned over on his back, and became unmanageable, and drifted ashore, where I found him. So I might give him a new name and call him a gull fish, but he is a useless fish and has no brains.

You have read the Jonah fish story in your Bible,

but it is not very correctly given in that book; so I am making no comments on it.

But here is another fish story which probably you think is a true one.

It looks very plausible, as Peter was a great fisherman. He was commanded to go and catch a fish and take money from its mouth and pay their taxes with it.

That does not seem a miracle to me, that a fish was caught with money in its mouth by as expert a fisherman as Peter was said to be.

I have caught hundreds of fish with coined money in their mouths, both Spanish and American coin, and made use of the said money. I don't know as I exactly paid taxes with it, but it was good for that.

But I was a fisherman much longer than Peter was, and never left my trade to fish for men as he did.

As fish stories are so marvellous I think it best not to tell any more, and if any one doubts the truth of any of my fish stories if he will come to me I will explain how it was done, and prove that all I have written on that subject is strictly true.

CHAPTER XXV.

MOSES made one mistake. His acts, as written by himself, were not mistakes. His ambition was to control the Israelites, and he accomplished it for a time by the aid of his brother Aaron ; and when he could not control them any longer he took the gold calf, with the pretence of going up the mountain to inquire of the Lord what to do, and when he got over the mountain he skipged with the calf, and did not leave anything behind him, not even his clothing.

So the old preachers declared that he had gone to heaven, clothes and all. And ministers preach it to-day. This is where the mistake is (not in Moses).

I consider him to have been a shrewd man, learned, level-headed, with power to deceive.

But I don't say what I think of men to-day who will preach that men go up to heaven alive, with there old clothes on, as they say Enoch and Moses did.

This is too much gospel for the nineteenth century, and will be fully ignored in the United States in the twentieth century, when the theological scales drop from men's eyes. (Satan's reign is nearly ended.)

Then they will see the fraud that has been practiced by the old Jewish priests. Rabbi Solomon Schindler don't speak very well of them.

I have told you several times that Moses never wrote the books ascribed to him, giving an account of the second creation, so freely credited to him; nor did he write the first chapter of Genesis, which describes another creation, wholly and entirely different from the second.

I will here note some of the differences of those two creations as given in the Bible, from internal evidence that cannot lie.

In the first creation the writer says that God created man in his own image, male and female, and commanded them to multiply, and gave them dominion over everything, and all animals, fishes and vegetables should be to eat. (Scientific.)

In the second creation the writer says the Lord God created man before the lower order. (Unscientific.)

This Adam was a know-nothing, and did not know what to eat. So the Lord told the scribe to tell him what to eat, and what not to eat.

I will mention some of those things that he was forbidden to eat:

Of animals the swine or hog and the bear are very good meat and previously allowed by God. And of fish thou shalt not eat the swordfish, it is not a true fish (cartilagenous); nor the dog fish, but the catfish you can eat. And the ink or cuttlefish (mollusk) thou shalt not eat. The fishermen call them squid.

The crustacean and bivalve the Israelites were not forbidden to eat. I give these latter names because those learned professors are more familiar with them than they would be with our fishermen's names. We are not familiar with each other's names, as I know some species to have four or five names that they are known by in different localities.

We are not a learned lot of men, and no doubt you wonder why Jesus should choose such men to found his Father's gospel on. As I know the reason why they were the best adapted to spread the true gospel I will refer to it when I get down to Jesus' time.

Jesus was a true reformer, but the people were ignorant and had to be deceived in order to be led as they always had been by Moses.

So he said he had come to fulfil the law and make and end of it. (A very polite way of condemning it.)

He often referred to the law, and said that he was the chief for whom they had been looking to redeem them from the Roman bondage.

He was a wise leader, and claimed that he would receive power from his Father in heaven to do it.

Jesus did not believe in the Mosaic creation at all, but condemned it in every essential part, and agreed with the first creation as I have given it to you, which was substantially as follows:

First, that the children of men were the sons of God, and that they had a right to everything on the earth for their use. and that all days were made for man. The Sabbath was made for man, and not man for the Sabbath, as Moses had declared; and that man was free and could not be the property of another man and entailed down to his heirs as property forever, as Moses had declared, and that every man who was hungry was entitled to all the corn he could eat, whether it was Sunday or Monday, no matter who planted the corn.

Moses called that the accursed thing, to take corn that others had planted and eat it, especially on the Sabbath, which he denounced as dreadful wicked, and to defend themselves for so doing was unpardonable.

Jesus instructed Peter when he was hungry to arise against oppression, slay and eat, and to call nothing unclean that God had made. Everything was good.

So you see that Jesus belongs to the first creation, and the only true one.

He also declared that he was God manifest in the flesh. (So were they, but they were too weak to receive such good news.)

But he was defeated by the Romans in his march on the Mount of Olives, from where he intended to go into Jerusalem in disguise, only five furlongs distance.

Had Jesus gained the day there would have been no Mosaic doctrine preached to-day. There would not be even a grease spot of that barbarous and cruel and false Judaism left, for he intended to wipe out slavery and destroy that curse, justified by the old law of Moses, called the law of God, I mean the Southerners' God.

They were honest and thought their slaves were

their property, and guaranteed by the God of Moses.

And how can you blame them?

They were very religious people, our brothers and Mosiac Christians.

This is just what Jesus told the Jews, that if they held on to the old Mosiac law it would make a wrangling in the family, and they would take up the sword and shed blood, and they did it with a vengeance.

I am sorry, yea, more than sorry, for it would have prevented that wicked rebellion, and we should not have had the dreadful results of that cruel and foolish war resting on us.

It makes my heart bleed as it were to think of it. In 1857 I stated in a public discussion in Provincetown, Mass., that there would be a serious rebellion and war in this country, such as had not been seen for many years, and that it would come inside of ten years and that the pretext would be slavery.

But the real cause was the misinterpretation of the Old and New Testaments, they being antagonistic, and both claiming to be the word of God.

The Southern people claimed the God of Moses.

The Northern people advocated the gospel as taught by Jesus.

And both would surely fight to enforce their own belief.

Now we all know, or ought to know, that our Federal Constitution guarantees to us religious liberty, but the people don't get it.

Better than that, we discard the Moses gospel of a multiplicity of wives. Solomon had seven hundred, and was not satisfied with even that number. He was called a wise man.

Our congressmen would not allow poor Brigham Young to have even forty when it was his privilege to have as many as he could take care of.

They said it was not moral, and passed a vote that a man should have only one wife, and then provided for its enforcement.

This was not according to the Constitution, but thought to be better morals.

I have told you about the South. Their religion did not suit us. So we declared "home rule," and sustained it. Good for us, and for Jesus.

Our predecessor declared it, but, like Parnell, he did not accomplish it. There was too much ignorance, superstition and priestcraft.

But our prototype told his followers that all the mighty works he did they should do, yea, more.

And we have done them. So that prophecy is fulfilled.

We have now said that the Chinese should not come because they would not give up their law giver and Ching-Ching for our Joss. We will allow no more to come, but will drive away all that are here unless they will give up their Joss and Ching-Ching for ours and become citizens.

This seems rather cruel in a country which tolerates religious liberty, or pretends to (but it is over the left).

We are following Jesus quite close. He forbid marriage altogether, until he should have accomplished his purpose, as women and children would be an

196

incumbrance to them in their fight for liberty and manliness; but then they should have one wife each.

Then he would reign or rule and they should snow down purely on mankind, as his father intended from the beginning.

Jesus was not opposed to women. It was Paul, or Saul, that wicked Jewish boy bachelor and free lover, who kept a woman at Damascus.

Jesus loved the girls, that is he loved Martha and Mary. At least your book says he did.

Now don't mix the two men together. One is of the old school, and the other of the new.

Paul would be tolerated by some of the preachers were he here to-day.

But Jesus would sit with us in state. And the priests of the Levites and the deacons of this world would pass by on the other side, and let us take care of bleeding humanity.

My dear friends, don't let Jewish Christians deceive you. Jesus has laid the foundation stone anew, and no other foundation shall any other man lay that will be a success.

There is a set of men who have that old brazen serpent of Moses coiled away and ready for use when the proper time comes.

Let me cry Woe, Woe, unto Croison. Woe unto Bethesda. Woe unto Sodom and Gomorrah. Woe unto Jerusalem. We have got the golden calf, and the God of power is on our side.

As Moses lifted up the serpent in the wilderness so has the son of man been lifted up and down, but the days of their deception are numbered. Jesus is

197

authority. He said his followers could take up serpents, and if they drank the deadly poison (that is, Judaism) it would not hurt them.

All we who have received the gifts by the laying on of hands, the love of man to man.

But I am inclined to think there are those who know better than they act.

> The morning light is breaking,
> The star has arisen in the West,
> We have nothing to fear,
> Our God and Humanity,
> Our Christ, will prevail,
> The wicked will cease from troubling us
> And the weary will be at rest.

This ode is dedicated to the wise by the author, J. A., the old fisherman.

According to the promise I will now give my learned friends a short sketch of Jesus, their would-be Saviour had he conquered the Romans and liberated his people and taught them the new life.

Jesus was of the tribe of Judah.

As a young man he was bold, ambitious, and in wisdom far surpassed all others of his day and time.

He was a friend of the poor man and common laborer.

He was death to aristocracy and priestcraft.

He taught his followers to call no man master. All were as brothers of a common family.

Jesus of the tribe of Judah, John of the tribe of Levi as the alias, and Christ put forth an effort to liberate the Jews from Roman bondage.

They claimed to have a message from God, that is the true God.

John, being a priest, well versed in the scriptures, could draw the common people after him.

He figured largely in upper Galilee, and instituted the temperance pledge and caused all to sign it, so they could be trusted.

Jesus, knowing where to find bold and resolute men, went down to Tiberus, in lower Galilee. He enlisted Pestus the governer, and Justus the warrior, or general, in his favor, and then went among the fishermen of Tiberus and along the coast of Galilee and called the fishermen and common laborers, and raised an army of thirty thousand soldiers.

And Peter, as he called him, was their leader. This Peter was Simon of the tribe of Zebulon, who was called the son of Thunder by his brethren, because he went off on the water and attacked big fish.

He had courage. He could fight, or fish for men.

Now, when the passover was about to come Jesus chose the most resolute and trusty of his men to secure weapons and follow him up to Jerusalem as though to worship God.

But Felix, the governor, feared there might be trouble, and being informed by an apostate Jew of the circumstance got his army in order and attacked Jesus on the Mount of Olives, and defeated him, and slew many and captured a number of prisoners.

Jesus and all who could run away, and boarded ships which took them safely to Tiberus. That ended his campaign in Jerusalem, his subsequent battles being fought in Galilee. He was the principal cause of the last war between the Jews and the Romans, which terminated so disastrously to them.

Men have got so much learning to-day and use so many useless words that even a eunuch could not understand without a Philip to act as interpreter. I will give you a sample.

God said: "Let there be light."

But the learned can flourish it off with the following words:

"How wonderful! Deity commanded that there should be light. That fair, first born of nature, should spring into existence with its almighty fiat. Light was ushered in from the womb of eternal darkness to enlighten this terrestrial ball with its glance of effulgence." Hear, hear.

And again we have it. The gunner went shooting birds; or, the sportsman shot a jay.

How sublime the following is:

"The sportsman observed the feathered rover; he lifts his gun, and sends the blow; swifter than a whirlwind flies the leaden death and lays the simple creature breathless on the ground."

The bird is dead! So be it. So be it.

Who was Jesus?

He was a reformer, and taught the true relationship of man to God, or the gods who created him, our Father who rules in the heavens.

Jesus was a believer in the first creation which I have described, and endeavored to convince his people that his father god was Love, and not angry with the people every day as Moses taught.

He condemned every essential point of the Mosaic

scriptures, and branded Moses as a fraud. I have no need to quote from the records. You have them, and can examine for yourselves.

But I will compare their doctrines, and leave you to decide.

Moses says "an eye for an eye," and "a tooth for a tooth," and "whosoever sheddeth man's blood by man shall his blood be shed." Retaliation with a vengeance.

But Jesus says, "Resist not evil," or, in other words, render not evil for evil. If you are compelled to go one mile, go two.

Moses commands a strict observance of the Sabbath, not even allowing the people to defend themselves on that day.

Jesus taught that all days were alike, and that the Sabbath was made for man, not man for the Sabbath, as Moses taught; and that it was right for his followers to pluck and eat the corn on that day, and not the accursed thing that Moses had described.

Moses forbid eating certain kinds of food. (That was good.)

Jesus made no restrictions, but told Peter to eat just what he wanted, if he could get it.

Moses taught the priest and Levite deacon to attend their meetings, and let the wounded lay for somebody else to care for.

But Jesus acknowledged as his brother the Samaritan who did the right thing.

Moses recommended slavery, and gave his people the right to buy and sell and own men and women as property and entail it to their posterity forever.

Jesus says man shall not hold property in man.

Moses says, "servants, obey your masters."

Jesus says, "call no man master. On earth all ye are brethren,"

Moses gives license to have as many wives as you want. Those who had the most were the wisest men. Solomon and David were noted examples.

Jesus forbid marriage, and told Peter to leave his wife and follow him, or he could not be his disciple.

Jonah says God prepared a fish to swallow him.

Matthew says Jonah was in the whale's belly three days and three nights.

Now you know a whale is not a fish.

There is no agreement between the old and new testaments, except that which is forced that the scriptures might seem to agree.

Moses demanded of the people one-tenth of all they earned for the priests, and an extra bullock, sheep and lamb, three of the best of the flock for the Lord God's share.

So Moses and Aaron, with their gilded calf and serpent and imaginary lord god, fleeced and enslaved the people.

Jesus says, "take neither purse nor scrip."

Paul says to the Corinthians: "Have I made gain of you? Hath Timothy or Philemon charged you anything for their services or preaching? Has not my gospel been free?"

John the Baptist forbid the use of wine and liquor.

Jesus forbid nothing that was good, but said if any man became intoxicated he could not be his disciple, nor could he enter the kingdom of heaven.

Paul wrote to his son Timothy to drink no more water, but use or drink wine for the stomach's sake.

Those three were triune teachers.

But I leave it with you to reconcile their teachings.

Consistency, thou art a jewel.

Jesus taught manliness triumphant.

And we have it now.

CHAPTER XXVI

IN closing this book I will give my Christian friends a specimen of the writing of the first three Christian fathers, which will probably be new to many of them. I am reminded of this as I happened to be in a Sunday School where a reverend gentleman was teaching a Bible class concerning the origin of the Christian Scriptures.

He said there was nothing authentically known about them until the fourth century.

So for the benefit of my readers I will copy from the first three centuries letters, communications and lamentations that have in them internal evidence of being written at that early period.

They are purely Christian, without any mixture of Judaism, written before your Bible was, which contains two parts Judaism, one part Romanism, one part Egyptianism or Monkish Christianity, with a little Greek.

And if the following named writers are not acknowledged as Christian writers then I must say there are none: Ignatius of the first century, who wrote a letter to the Virgin Mary, as given in a previous chapter ; Justin Martyr, who sent a petition to Cæsar, A. D. 141 ; and Origen. who wrote his lamentations in the third century.

The foregoing contain only one reference to Judaism, and constitute what has since been called Christianity, but is mostly Judaism of to-day.

That Judaism caused the rebellion in 1861, and prompted the trouble with the Mormons.

In Origen's lamentations you have a fac-simile of Job's lamentations written without Judaism originally, long before that wonderful lamentation of unhappy Jeremiah.

Those lamentations will compare favorably with those embodied in Young's " Night Thoughts," or perhaps still better, those set forth in Milton's " Paradise Lost," where Adamology is illustrated with a vengeance.

I am ready to declare boldly for Adam, and believe it was good for us that Adam ate the apple of knowledge that led him to be a farmer and gave him the ability to plant beans and how to mind and take care of his peas.

You will perceive that the book of Lamentations is a Jewish book, and refers to Job, or is taken from that book, and magnified, and the last part made to refer to the calamities of the Jewish people, or the destruction of Jerusalem.

This mingles Christianity with Judaism, and is passed off to-day as God's word and called the Christian Bible.

Let a clear and well-balanced mind read all those

records without prejudice and he will see that the writer of the book of Jeremiah gave himself away when he spoke of the people of Uz, that city of Job in Chaldea.

This book is a mixture of Judaism and Christianity, and was written in the fourth century by the order of Constantine and placed where such records did not belong, like many other books of the Bible, written without date or locality, and having attached to them fictitious names of persons as authors.

Of all this the book mentioned gives ample evidence.

I would not give my honest friends anything but absolute truth, well authenticated with internal evidence that cannot lie.

Those books are given as God's word to the Jews, and my learned friends must be aware that there are no absolutely true histories in existence.

I think Josephus wrote as true and impartial a history as was ever written, but it has been much changed, so that to day it cannot be understood by its readers in general, unless they understand electro-psychology and have no axe to grind.

I am struck with wonder and amazement when I read the holy scriptures as it were.

Luke, when describing the birth of Jesus, in the thirty-fifth verse of the first chapter, does not call him a child or baby, but a holy thing; and Milton has the same account in such language as this: "Dovelike sat brooding on the vast abyss and made it pregnant." Paradise Lost, book 1.

I suppose my good Christian brothers and reverend gentlemen will skip that which does not accord with their previously conceived ideas, and accept only what agrees with their accepted notions.

But I am so unfortunately organized that I cannot accept anything but truth. I know it is not fashionable now.

For the following petition and lamentation I am indebted to the learned author of the Digest, Rev. Robert Taylor, A. B., F. R. S., of Cambridge College, England.

In giving records written by our forefathers I do not say much about Constantine, as all Christians must be familiar with them. Let this suffice:

" Having by God's assistance gotten the victory over mine enemies I entreat you therefore, beloved ministers of God and servants of our Lord and Saviour Jesus Christ, to cut off the heads of this hydra of heresy, for so shall ye please both God and me."

This much says the founder of our Christianity.

But murder will out.

Dr. Lardner, that eminent Christian divine, says of Constantine, his work, in volume two, page 342:

He put to death:

Maximian,	His wife's father - - - -	A. D. 310
Bassianus,	His sister Anastasia's husband	314
Licinianus,	His nephew, by Constantia	319
Fausta,	His wife - - - - - -	320
Sopater,	His former friend - - -	321
Licinius,	His sister Constantia's husband	325
Crispus,	His own son - - - - -	326

I feel it a duty I owe to the community to give them the character of the founder of Christianity

as portrayed by a noted Christian author, and take
Justin Martyr's address in the year 141 from
Gibbons' writings:

"Unto the Autocrat Titus Ælius Adrianus; unto
Antonius Pius, most noble Cæsar and true Philosopher; unto Lucius, son of the philosopher Cæsar, and
adopted of Pius, favorers of learning; and unto the
sacred Senate, with all the people of Rome; on the
behalf of those persons who, among all sorts of men,
are unjustly hated and reproached: I, Justin, the
son of Priscus Bacchius of Flavia Neapolis, of Pales-
tine in Syria, as one of their number, do, suppliant
with earnest prayers, present this my petition"—
(omissis omittendis)—"You hold not the scales of
Justice even; for, instigated by headstrong passions,
and driven on also by the invisible whips of evil
demons, you take great care that we shall suffer
though your care not for what.

"For verily I must tell you that heretofore those
impure spirits under various apparitions went into
the daughters of men, and defiled boys, and dressed
up such scenes of horror that such as entered not
into the reason of things, but judged by appearance
only, stood aghast at the spectres; and being shrunk
up with fear and amazement, and never imagining
them to be devils, called them gods, and invoked
them by such titles as each devil was pleased to
nickname himself by.

"If then we hold some opinions near of kin to
the poets and philosophers in greatest repute among
you, why are we thus unjustly hated? For, in saying that all things were made in this beautiful order

by God, what do we seem to say more than Plato? When we teach general conflagration, what do we teach more than Stoics? By opposing the worship of the works of men's hands, we concur with Meander the comedian; and by declaring the Logos the first begotten of God, our Master Jesus Christ, to be born of a Virgin without any human mixture, and to be crucified and dead, and to have risen again, and ascended into heaven, we say no more in this than what you say of those whom you style the Sons of Jove.

"For you need not be told what a parcel of sons the writers most in vogue among you assign to Jove. There's Mercury, Jove's interpreter, in imitation of the Logos, in worship among you. There's Æsculapius, the physician, smitten by a bolt of thunder, and after that ascending into heaven. There's Bacchus torn to pieces, and Hercules burnt to get rid of his pains. There's Pollux and Castor, the sons of Jove by Leda, and Perseus by Danae. Not to mention others, I would fain know why you always deify the departed Emperors, and have a fellow at hand to make affidavit that he saw Cæsar mount to heaven from the funeral pile. As to the son of God, called Jesus, should we allow him to be nothing more than man, yet the title of the Son of God is very justifiable upon the account of his wisdom, considering you have your Mercury in worship, under the title of the Word and Messenger of God.

" As to the objection to our Jesus' being crucified, I say that suffering was common to all the fore-mentioned sons of Jove, but only they suffered another kind of death. As to his being born of a virgin, you have your Perseus to balance that. As to his curing the lame, and the paralytic, and such as were cripples from their birth, this is little more than what you say of your Æsculapius.

"But if the Christian profession must still meet with such bitter treatment, remember what I told you before, that the farthest you can go is to take away our lives, but the loss of this life will certainly be no ill bargain to us; but you indeed, and all such wicked enemies without repentance, shall one day dearly pay for this persecution in fire everlasting. And as far as these things shall appear agreeable to truth, so far we would desire you to respect 'em accordingly; but if they seem trifling, despise them as trifles; however, don't proceed against the professors of them, who are people of the most inoffensive lives, as severely as against your professed enemies. For tell you I must, that if you persist in this course of iniquity, you shall not escape the vengeance of God in the other world."

The lamentation of Origen:

"In bitter affliction and grief of mind, I address myself unto them which hereafter shall read me thus confoundedly. But how can I speak with tongue tied, with throat dammed up, and lips that refuse their office. I fall to the ground on my bare knees and make this my humble prayer and supplication unto all the saints, that they will help me, silly wretch that I am, who by reason of the superfluity of my sin, dare not look up unto God. O ye saints of the blessed God! with watery eyes and sodden cheeks soaked in grief and pain, I beseech you to fall down before the mercy-seat of God for me, miserable sinner. Woe is me, because of the sorrow of my heart! Woe is me for affliction of my soul. Woe is me, O my mother, that ever thou broughtest me forth, an heir of the kingdom of God, but now become an inheritor of the kingdom of the Devil; a perfect man, yea a priest, yet found wallowing in impurity; a man beautified with honor and dignity, yet in the end blemished with ignominy and shame; a burning light, yet forthwith darkened; a running fountain, yet by and by dried up; O who will give streams of tears unto mine eyes, that I may bewail my sorrowful plight : O my lost priesthood! O my dishonored ministry; O all you, my friends, tender my case! Pity me, O all ye, my friends, in that I have now trodden under foot the seal and cognizance of my profession, and joined league with the devil! Pity me, O ye, my friends, in that I am rejected and cast away from the face of God. It is for my lewd life that I am thus polluted, and noted with open shame. Alas, how am I fallen. Alas, how am I thus come to nought! There is no sorrow comparable unto my sorrow; there is no affliction that exceedeth my affliction; there is no lamentation more lamentable than mine ; neither is there any sin greater than my sin ; and there is no salve for me. Alas! O father Abraham! entreat for me, that I be not cut off from thy coast. Rid me, O Lord, from the roaring lion! The whole assembly of saints doth make intercession unto thee for me. The whole choir of angels do entreat thee for me. Let down upon me thy Holy Spirit, that with his fiery countenance he may put to flight the crooked fiends of the devil! Let me be received again into the joy of my God, through the prayers and intercessions of the saints, through the earnest petitions of the Church which sorroweth over me, and humbleth herself unto Jesus Christ; to whom, with the Father and the Holy Ghost, be all glory and honor, for ever and ever. Amen." So far Origen shows his insanity.

I have abridged this intolerably tedious farrago, without breaking a single sentence, or changing or supplying one word not authorized by the original text.

The most distinguished of all the works of Origen is his celebrated answer to Celsus, contained in eight books.

Sketch of Constantine:

Eusebius Pamphilus, who has written his life, seems to know no bounds of exaggeration in his praise. "I am amazed" (says this veracious bishop, on whose fidelity all our knowledge of ecclesiastical antiquity must ultimately depend), "I am amazed, when I contemplate such singular piety and goodness. Moreover when I look up to heaven, and in my mind behold his blessed soul living in God's presence, and there invested (crowned) with a blessed and unfading wreath of immortality; considering this, I am oppressed with silent amazement, and my weakness makes me dumb, resigning his due encomium to Almighty God, who alone can give to Constantine the praise he merits.

"Constantine alone, of the Roman emperors, was

beloved of God, and hath left us the idea of his most pious and religious life as an inimitable example for other men to follow, at an humble distance.

"Constantine was the first of all the emperors who was regenerated by the new birth of baptism, and signed with the sign of the cross; and being thus regenerated, his mind was so illuminated, and by the raptures of faith so transported, that he admired in himself the wonderful work of God; and when the centurions and captains, admitted to his presence, did bewail and mourn for his approaching death, because they should lose so good and gracious a prince, he answered them, 'that he only now began to live, and that he now only began to be sensible of happiness, and therefore he now only desired to hasten, rather than to slack or stay, his passage to God.'

"For he alone of all the Roman emperors did, with most religious zeal, honor and worship God. He alone, with great liberty of speech, did profess the gospel of Jesus Christ. He alone, did honor his church more than all the rest. He alone, abolished the wicked adoration of idols; and, therefore, he alone, both in his life and after death, hath been crowned with such honors as no one hath obtained, neither among the Grecians nor Barbarians, nor in former times, among the Romans. Since no age hath produced anything that might be paralleled or compared to Constantine. So much for his praise!

"The adulation of interested sycophants, and the applause of priests and bishops, will not erase the more convincing evidence of those stubborn things, facts, that will not be suppressed, and cannot lie. Even Lardner, who omits entirely the circumstances of aggravation, acknowledges the deeds, which give a very different complexion to Constantine's character, from that, which the honor of Christianity requires that it should wear. The hireling voice of priestcraft would extol him to the skies. Nor ought we, in judging of the worth of a churchman's panegyric, to forget that even the cautious and ingenuous Lardner, who has, without evidence of a single act of wrong against him, branded the amiable and matchlessly virtuous Julian as a persecutor, has not one ill word to spare for the Christian Constantine, who drowned his unoffending wife, Fausta, in a bath of boiling water, beheaded his eldest son, Crispus, in the very year in which he presided in the Council of Nice, murdered the two husbands of his sisters, Constantia and Anastasia, murdered his own nephew, being his sister Constantia's son, a boy only twelve years old, and murdered a few others,* which actions, Lardner, with truly Christian moderation, tells us, 'seem to cast a reflection upon him.' Among those few others, never be it forgotten, was Sopater, the Pagan priest, who fell a victim and a

---

*His slaughter bill, methodically arranged, runs thus :

Maximian,	His wife's father - - - - A. D.	310
Bassianus,	His sister Anastasia's husband	314
Licinianus,	His nephew, by Constantia	319
Fausta,	His wife - - - - - -	320
Sopater,	His former friend - - - -	321
Licinius,	His sister Constantia's husband	325
Crispus	His own son - - - - -	326

martyr to the sincerity of his attachment to Paganism, and to the honesty of his refusing the consola-
tions of heathenism to the conscience of the royal
murderer.

"The death of Crispus (says Dr. Lardner) is
altogether without any good excuse; so likewise is
the death of the young Licinianus, who could not
then be more than a little over eleven years of age,
and appears not to have been charged with any
fault, and can hardly be suspected of any."*

* Lardner, vol. 2, p. 342.